HEAT

Series 3 Number 11

Ruark Lewis
The Intro (Or Don't You Have a Phone?) 2019
pencil, pen and ink on paper
25 × 19 cm
courtesy of the artist

Sydney artist Ruark Lewis is widely
recognised for his works which
involve a reworking of literary,
musical and archival art texts – in
this case, transcription drawings
from *the use* (2017, www.theuse.info)
by the late Chris Mann.

'A transcription,' he says, 'is to cut
or move across, to go beyond, or
pass over. So if I draw the sound of
words, first faintly outlined in pencil
(with that trace the voice remains),
then further my nib dipped in the
ink reforms the body, like a figure or
character standing on the lines,
then I finely mask (with another layer
of pen work) the lyric vocal impulse
of the performer Chris Mann and
what remains is a disguise made up
of haptic shapes and a memory that
represents the rhythmic form of
his spirit.'

EVELYN JUERS
TOTALITY IN WALLAL.
WOOLF IN YORKSHIRE.
EINSTEIN IN SCHARBEUTZ.

Evelyn Juers is an art and literary
critic, essayist, Brontë and biography
scholar, and the author of *House of
Exile* (2008), *The Recluse* (2012) and
The Dancer (2021).

MORE THAN OTHER GENRES, biography defies methodology. So how do we read it? Compliantly, absorbing psychological insights, historical context, for entertainment, to discover how a life was lived? Or pushing back, interpretively, digressively, reading between lines, working with but also against the subject, the author, the biographical imperative? This is an essay on the second 'method', hardly a method at all, rather a walk on some biographical byways, a personalised itinerary.

Asking 'How should one read a book?' in *The Common Reader*, Virginia Woolf advises relatively, that *even if I could answer the question for myself, the answer would apply only to me and not to you.* The essay was delivered on 30 January 1926 as a talk to teenage girls at Hayes Court Common school in Kent. She had been invited by Katherine A. Cox, the school's Harvard- and McGill-educated headmistress and English teacher. It was a cold, wet day; the students sat on the carpet of the school's drawing room, visitors and staff sat around the fire, and Woolf *at a little table near the piano. She wore a bright blue polo-necked jersey... she made a striking figure*, one student recalled, while another thought it was all *very boring* (*Hayseed to Harvest*). Perhaps to add a little spark, Woolf suggested that some books *are suitable for the bath, requiring the minimum effort of comprehension.*

She recommends reading *lives and letters, because we can make them light up the many windows of the past; we can watch the famous dead in their familiar habits and fancy sometimes that we are very close and can surprise their secrets.* Drawn to biography, she was also uncertain about its status. In 'The Art of Biography' she calls it *a young art*, compared to poetry and fiction. I'd argue that it is no mere eighteenth- or nineteenth-century fledgling, but the most ancient of literary phenomena, the super-genre from which all others spring. In fact, Woolf's own diary – she calls it *rough and random* – became the very best of her work, an urgent, vital, panoptic auto/biographical masterpiece.

Like all great books, great biography comes in different sizes. Giorgio Vasari's *Lives of the Artists* and Lytton Strachey's *Eminent Victorians* are miniature gems. Elizabeth Gaskell's *The Life of Charlotte Brontë* and Janet Malcolm's double portrait of Sylvia Plath and Ted Hughes are feisty classics, medium-sized. On the next steps up, however – the tome, the brick, the boulder, the spine-breaker – we encounter wonders on another scale: James Boswell's voracious Johnson, Alan Schom's problematic Napoleon (Schom dislikes his subject), Richard Holmes's all-round Romantics Shelley and Coleridge, Lyndall Gordon's volcanic Emily Dickinson, Michael Holroyd's ironic Strachey, Klaus Harpprecht's mega-Mann (Thomas, sustained for over two thousand pages across two volumes), Hermione Lee's definitive Woolf, Carole Angier's closely scrutinised Sebald, Hazel Rowley's homely-worldly Christina Stead, or in a collective memoir, Alexis Wright's heroic Tracker Tilmouth. Those large biographies differ from the heigh-ho lives crowding bookshop shelves. They are monuments not only for their scope, their star subjects, and their wealth of scholarship, but for their literary qualities, which means readers engage with the writer's writerliness.

Reading oversized literary biographies of around six hundred or more pages is slow and immersive. There's space for us (if we take the time) to explore. While Leon Edel's massive Henry James spent a year on my bedside table, I also veered towards his friend Edith Wharton, her houses, gardens, travels, the genius of her work. When Carole Angier revealed that the real-life models for

Sebald's fictions were very angry with him for his appropriations of their stories, I applauded her for her investigations. At the end of Hazel Rowley's biography of Christina Stead – with Stead living in a tiny room in a large Gothic mansion in Sydney, drinking a daily bottle or two of Cinzano Rosso, as *her past unreeled before her* – I began to revisit Stead's work and Stead's Sydney.

Traversing terrain-like biographies is slower still if the reader stops to check something. Almost like a writer – but without the constraints – we make notes, visit libraries, get up to *follow in the footsteps of*...and drift. Our interest might shift from Napoleon's wars to his paranoias to the paranoias of other despots. Or from Boswell's Johnson back to Boswell. How to define this kind of activity? The drift, it seems, is not quite the *dérive*. It would be clumsy to call the experience of reading very large literary biographies *psychogeographical*. Although – if we take psychogeography as spontaneous methods of observation which activate subtexts and create connections, and if step by step, word by word, walking and reading are akin – then it is something like that, of things coming unexpectedly into view.

In her how-to essay, Woolf concurs: *Is there not an open window on the right hand of the bookcase? How delightful to stop reading and look out! How stimulating the scene is... The greater part of any library is nothing but the record of such fleeting moments...vanished moments and forgotten lives.* Elsewhere she likens large biographies to feasts full of *hints and glimpses* ('The Modern Essay').

Elements that slip through the biographical mesh and wink from below resemble Guy Debord's 'microclimates', Georges Perec's 'infraordinary', Edith Wharton's 'incidents', Woolf's 'small' things or 'diamonds of the dustheap'. They have weight, they are not ephemera. Examined more closely, they shed light on the person or group of people being portrayed. For instance, in reading about – and around – Albert Einstein (initially as research for *House of Exile*), I was intrigued by three localities, Wallal on the coast of Western Australia, Yorkshire in Northern England, and Scharbeutz on the Baltic Sea. Wallal (it seems to me) is a place of great importance in the Einstein story. Yorkshire links him with the literary world. And in Scharbeutz we find him in a quiet seaside village, resting. None of them appear in his major biographies, perhaps because in two of those places he is not 'on stage', and in one he is on holiday.

Einstein is one of the most celebrated people in history, he has 'name recognition', as it's called in the biography industry. His story is told and retold, abbreviated, elaborated, thematised, fictionalised. There are chunky biographies as well as slimmer, more specialised studies, of Einstein the scientist, the peacenik, the rebel, the refugee, the cosmic engineer, books on Einstein's Berlin, interviews with his housekeeper, his theories of relativity (and infidelity), the young genius (scorned), husband, father, joker, the German-Swiss-American, his Jewish identity, his FBI file, his stolen brain. There's a biography devoted entirely to his famous equation. *Einstein on the Beach* is an opera by Philip Glass. There are films, comics, games, dolls, wigs, and legal disputes about merchandise. A shy person, he never liked the celebrity cult which enlisted him. He said fame made him stupid.

He was born on 14 March 1879 in Ulm, a southern town of the newly formed but already heavily militarised German Empire. He spent his childhood in Munich, lived in Pavia, Zürich, Aarau, Bern, Prague, Berlin and Princeton, and travelled widely, in

Europe, Asia, the Middle East, and North and South America.

As a child he learned to play the violin, becoming an accomplished and passionate musician who preferred Mozart and Bach to Beethoven. From his earliest years he questioned authority and his formal education was fragmented. He left school at the age of fifteen to join his family in Italy, hiked in the Alps and Apennines, and finished his education in Switzerland at a school based on Pestalozzi's pedagogical principles. There he learned visual and spatial thinking, which helped him formulate his scientific theories. To avoid military service, he renounced his German citizenship in 1896. Around that time too he read the science and fiction of Aaron Bernstein, which fired his imagination.

From 1896 until 1900 he attended ETH, the Zürich Polytechnic. In his spare time he sailed on Alpine lakes. In 1901 he gained Swiss citizenship. In 1903 he married Mileva Marić, a fellow student, mathematician and physicist. They shared research interests and a love of music; they had three children together, Lieserl born illegitimately in 1902 (and put up for adoption), Hans Albert in 1904, Eduard in 1910. One of her biographers describes Marić as *the mathematical heart of a startling revolution in physics*; it's a tragedy that family commitments soon undercut her studies and career. From 1902 until 1909 Einstein worked at the Swiss Patent Office in Bern, testing electromechanical inventions. With his best friends, mathematician Marcel Grossmann and engineer Michele Besso, he formed a reading group, the Olympia Academy; they discussed science and philosophy and literary classics. David Hume's scepticism and Baruch Spinoza's humanism were lasting influences. Cervantes's *Don Quixote* was a constant companion. Years later he would tell his sister Maja that *Don Quixote* had always been his favourite book, next to the Bible. He was deeply impressed by Dostoevsky's *The Brothers Karamazov*.

When he produced four important papers in 1905, he was still an unknown patent clerk. The first paper was 'On a Heuristic Point of View Concerning the Production and Transformation of Light'. The second was 'On the Movement of Small Particles Suspended in Stationary Liquids Required by the Molecular-Kinetic Theory of Heat'. The third was 'On the Electrodynamics of Moving Bodies', asking how speed affects mass, time and space and introducing Einstein's 'Special Theory of Relativity'. The fourth was 'On the Mass-Energy Equivalent', asking whether the inertia of a body depends on its energy content, and answering with the triumphant equation $E=mc^2$, where the energy of a body at rest equals its mass times the speed of light squared. Marić had checked and double-checked his calculations. 1905 is known as his miracle year. He was exhausted and went to bed for two weeks.

Wary of the papers' astonishing abstractions, some academics claimed they were based on 'Jewish' science. And although Max Planck, Europe's leading theoretical physicist, was one of his staunchest supporters, for some years Einstein struggled to obtain a university appointment. His PhD from the University of Zürich, titled 'A New Determination of Molecular Dimensions' and conferred in 1906, led at first to nothing more than a promotion from third- to second-class clerk at the patent office, a job he could not give up even when he was offered a low-paid position at the University of Bern. Always he was desperate for extra time to do his own work.

The offer of a position as Extraordinary Professor at the University of Zürich brought more antisemitism. In recommending Einstein for the job, Alfred Kleiner – Professor of

Physics and Einstein's PhD supervisor – felt he had to argue that while Einstein *happens to be a Jew* he did not display the typically *unpleasant peculiarities of [Jewish] character*.

Antisemitic opposition continued throughout his academic career and for this and other reasons he developed mixed feelings about academia. It happened again in 1911 at Prague's German University, where he was offered the Chair in Theoretical Physics. Franz Kafka attended one of his lectures and they met socially, but there was no rapport. Rumour has it that many years later Thomas Mann gave Einstein a copy of *The Castle*, but he returned it very quickly, saying he could not read it, because life was not that complicated. By the summer of 1912, Einstein and his family had returned to Zürich, for his appointment as Professor of Theoretical Physics. Marić had health problems, their marriage had broken down, and he had begun a relationship with his cousin Elsa Löwenthal. He was thirty-three, she was thirty-six.

Einstein was a pacifist. He disliked all forms of conflict, including chess. He believed internationalism could reduce the risks of nationalism and militarism. To protest against the barbarity of war, he signed The Manifesto to Europeans. But it was ineffective.

From 1914 until 1933 he held a professorship at the University of Berlin. Sometimes he went on holiday. He especially loved summers on the Baltic, where (according to artists who flocked there) water and light combine to create a special kind of atmospheric magic. In 1915, with Elsa and her teenage daughters Ilse and Margot, he rented an apartment in Haus Johanneshorst in Sellin on the windy island of Rügen. Once a popular resort, they had it almost to themselves, as the war kept holidaymakers away. They could walk on the pier, on beaches, and through a forest to Black Lake. If any of the island's trains were still running, they may have visited other places, the two lighthouses of Kap Arkona, or the Chalk Cliffs painted by Caspar David Friedrich. Around that time, Rügen was being set up as a transfer station for wounded prisoners of war. Einstein kept working, even on vacation.

With mathematical help from Marcel Grossmann, he had been refining his earlier calculations and now achieved his greatest breakthrough. On 25 November 1915 he submitted his General Theory of Relativity to the Prussian Academy of Sciences. It addressed the limitations of Isaac Newton's theories of fixed time and space and proposed that space-time is curved, gravity causes it to bend or warp, to wrap or roll around objects, that it is flexible. It was a dramatic moment in science, the universe opening up just as the human world threatened to collapse. 1915 was a gruesome year of trench warfare, immeasurable multitudes of dead and wounded, at Gallipoli, Ypres, the Masurian Lakes, and many other battlefields. German Zeppelin attacked Britain, German submarines sunk passenger ships, poison gas was used by both sides.

In the summer of 1918 for about seven weeks, he and Elsa and her daughters stayed a little further west along the Baltic coast, in Ahrenshoop, a charming village on a sandy promontory with sea on one side and a lagoon on the other. They rented rooms in the Old Customs House. In letters to friends and family he expressed the great joy of being far from big cities, far from the *so-called world*, without telephones, newspapers and responsibilities, in a place of *absolute tranquility*. Barefoot. Loafing. Anonymous. Thinking. Free of commitments like lecturing, which always made him uneasy, even sick. He described himself on the sunniest days, *lying on the shore like a crocodile*, getting a tan, reading among other things Immanuel Kant's *Prolegomena*. Fine reading, he called it, though he thought Kant showed less common sense than Hume. To one of his correspondents he quotes from *an exquisite little poem* by Heinrich Heine. As a keen sailor, attuned to waves and wind, he thought that here, in stormy weather, *the sea is magnificent*. But there were no sailboats for hire and he had to be satisfied, now and then, with being a passenger on a fishing boat. *An enviable existence...in glorious nature*, he told Max Planck. They were still in Ahrenshoop in early August, when the Allied Counteroffensive began on the Western Front.

After the war, the writer Romain Rolland's anti-war manifesto – the Declaration of the Independence of the Mind – was signed by Einstein, the artist Käthe Kollwitz, writers Hermann Hesse, Stefan Zweig and Heinrich Mann, photographer Alfred Stieglitz, philosopher Bertrand Russell, poet Rabindranath Tagore, and others. After being *kept apart for five years by the armies, the censorship and the mutual hatred of the warring nations*, they asked thinkers to reunite the world.

Einstein's call for astrophysicists to prove his theory of relativity had gone out in 1912. He needed them to photograph stars during a total solar eclipse – when the sun's light is briefly obstructed by the moon – then to develop the photographic plates, measure the stars' positions and compare these measurements with images of the same stars in a normal night sky. And although astronomers have always studied eclipses, Einstein's call introduced a new urgency – dubbed the Einstein problem – which resulted in four troubled expeditions. The first in 1912 in southeastern Brazil was directed by a young astronomer from the Berlin Observatory, Erwin Freundlich; it encountered bad weather. The second in 1914 in Crimea was directed collaboratively by Freundlich and William Wallace Campbell, head of the University of California's Lick Observatory; it met with the outbreak of WWI and heavy cloud. Freundlich was briefly arrested by the Russians and the astronomers' equipment was confiscated. Had those two tests succeeded, Einstein's career would have hit a hurdle, because his calculations required the adjustments he made in 1915 and published in March 1916 in *Annalen der Physik*, his 'General Theory of Relativity'.

Though the war prevented further expeditions, it did not stop the British astronomer Arthur Eddington in his promotion of Einstein's ideas, which captured the imaginations of many, including Virginia Woolf. She began writing her second novel *Night and Day* in mid-1916 and it was published in October 1918. She has her heroine (a mathematician and astronomer) and her hero in different places, but looking up at the same time at the same night sky, the heroine's *sight of the heavens...partially intercepted by the light leafless hoops of a pergola...a spray of clematis* obscuring the Milky Way. And at Christmas the *Heavens bend over the earth with sympathy*. In all her work, Woolf would keep testing the idea of relativity: through overlaps of time and space, contractions and expansions, deformations, pluralities, simultaneities, affinities.

The race to prove Einstein's theory resumed. First off the mark was Campbell, with the Lick Observatory's solar expedition in Washington State in June 1918; it failed because they were still waiting for the Russians to return their equipment and had to make do with inferior instruments. In 1919, also with old equipment but hoping for better luck, Eddington, accompanied by Edwin Cottingham, a clockmaker and expert in astronomical time-keeping, set out for the island of Príncipe off the African west coast. From the ship Eddington wrote to his mother: *It seems curious to have done with rationing entirely – [to have again] unlimited sugar, and large slices of meat, puddings with pre-war quantity of raisins and currants in them.* The team was directed (from Greenwich) by the Astronomer Royal, Frank Watson Dyson.

Despite the heat and humidity, Eddington thought the *very green* island of rainforest and cocoa, banana, breadfruit and coffee plantations, was charming. Everyone, from governor to judge to harbour master, was helpful; there were picnics, tennis matches, and musical evenings. He noted the beauty of butterflies and flavour of pineapples; regretted that sharks kept him from swimming. On the morning of the eclipse on 29 May it rained heavily. The sky cleared as if to tease the observers, before the clouds returned. Sixteen photographs were taken but Eddington himself admitted there was just *one good plate that I measured [which] gave a result agreeing with Einstein and I think I have a little confirmation from a second plate.* Simultaneously, an expedition in Sobral, northeastern Brazil, resulted in instrument and heat problems, blurry results, and measurements for only four or five stars, that differed from the results in Príncipe. It's still unclear to what extent these results were suppressed.

Eddington's presentation of his findings to the Royal Society and the Royal Astronomical Society, and their acceptance that this confirmed Einstein's theory, ensured international media coverage, public interest, and instant fame for Einstein. In London *The Times* called it a revolution in science. *The New York Times* ran this excited headline: *LIGHTS ALL ASKEW IN THE HEAVENS/ Men of Science More or Less Agog Over Results of Eclipse*

Observations/ EINSTEIN THEORY TRIUMPHS/ Stars Not Where They Seemed or Were Calculated to be, but Nobody Need Worry.

Pleased with the news, Einstein bought himself a new violin. He called all his violins Lina. And when asked to give a lecture, he sometimes played a Mozart sonata instead. That year, after his divorce from Mileva, he married Elsa, though by some accounts he also considered marrying her daughter Ilse. They chose the Baltic island of Hiddensee – between Rügen and Ahrenshoop – for their summer retreat.

When the architect Erich Mendelsohn was a German soldier on the eastern front, he made sketches for an Einstein Tower, an astrophysical observatory to keep testing Einstein's theories. In consultation with Freundlich, who designed the tower's telescope, and supported by private and state funding, and the Telegrafenberg in Potsdam chosen for its site, construction started in 1919. It was completed in 1924. Einstein thought this masterpiece of Expressionist architecture looked *organisch*.

Peace was overshadowed by memories of war. The influenza pandemic was in its third wave. The economy was weak. There were political uprisings and murders. People were on edge. Although the Treaty of Versailles held Germany accountable for the devastation it had caused, Jews were often blamed for ongoing instabilities. News of proof of Einstein's theory encountered both anti-German sentiment in countries like Belgium and anti-Jewish sentiment in sections of the German scientific community, where some accused Einstein of stealing an 'Aryan' idea proposed by a German astronomer. Hitler issued one of his earliest propaganda documents, on what he called the Jewish Question, declaring the *removal of the Jews altogether* as his *ultimate goal*. During lectures, Einstein was heckled by antisemitic students. In 1920, to protect him, some of his circle urged him to stop the publication of an interview-based biography by his friend Alexander Moszkowski, because it might attract more taunts. He seemed unruffled. His own strong identification with Judaism was one of kinship, not faith, and always, according to Walter Isaacson, *his allergy to nationalism kept him from being a pure and unalloyed Zionist.* Plagued by all kinds of public attention, good and bad, Einstein dreamed he was burning in hell and the postman, delivering ever-new requests, was the devil. But much as he loathed making appearances, he always rose to the occasion.

In 1921 he holidayed in Ahrenshoop and nearby Wustrow, and in Kiel with his sons. He enjoyed their company, pleased to find them healthy and intelligent, and to share with them his love of sailing. A non-swimmer, he was proud that his boys *swim about like whales.* He told their mother, *it really is nice to have such big boys.*

In Britain, while the Eddington experiment was widely lauded as proof of general relativity, it also caused controversy. Scientists debated the theory while not always understanding it, some admitting it was beyond their grasp. To stay ahead, the British were keen to confirm Eddington's results during the next solar eclipse. That is how it was put, as 'confirmation of Eddington's measurements', rather than further sets of independent observations to confirm Einstein's theory.

In America too, some of Campbell's colleagues thought Einstein's theory was *accursed* because it defied common sense. Campbell was anxious about it but managed to remain neutral, with an open mind, and his position was strengthened when Robert Trumpler, a Swiss-born astronomer with a better understanding of relativity, joined his preparations for 1922 in Wallal.

Hyperinflation spiralled out of control in Germany, partly due to the war reparations the country had to pay. Walther Rathenau, the German foreign minister and leading representative of the Weimar Republic, was blamed for his role in signing the Treaty of Versailles. He was assassinated on 24 June 1922. A million mourners attended his funeral. Rathenau was Einstein's friend. They had attended concerts together and read each other's work, Rathenau joking that Einstein's was *relatively* easy to understand. On some things they disagreed. Rathenau believed in assimilation as a counterforce to antisemitism, Einstein didn't. After the assassination, Einstein was warned he was the nationalists' next target. He moved to Kiel for a while and kept a low profile.

Knowing that he planned to visit Asia, and offering a generous honorarium and travel expenses, the universities of Sydney, Melbourne and Adelaide invited Einstein for September. He declined. He never came to Australia, but it might be said that he was in Wallal, in the minds of his scientific collaborators.

Traditionally owned by the Nyangumarta People, Wallal is situated on the border between the Pilbara and Kimberley regions, at Eighty (formerly Ninety) Mile Beach on the northwest coast of Australia, where the sun rises over the Great Sandy Desert and sets over the Indian Ocean.

It is a place of exceptional importance to Einstein's theory of general relativity. In September 1922 a solar eclipse was to begin in (what was then known as) Abyssinia, pass over the Indian Ocean, over Christmas Island, crossing the coast at Wallal, moving over other parts of Australia, departing the continent at Ballina on the east coast, and finishing north of New Zealand. Observation posts were set up along its path, but Wallal promised the best chance of clear skies and the longest duration of totality, estimated at five minutes and nineteen seconds.

Some British scientists considered Wallal *a hopeless place*. Opposition to sending a solar eclipse expedition to Wallal seemed to come mainly from the astronomer, cartographer and geographer Arthur Robert Hinks, famous for determining the distance between the sun and Earth. Since then, he confessed, astronomy had entered new theoretical territory, and relativity was not for him. He was also disappointed to have missed out on the directorship of the Cambridge Observatory, which went to Eddington. But encouraged by international interest in Wallal as a suitable site, Alexander D. Ross, Foundation Professor of Mathematics and Physics at the University of Western Australia, was one of a group who lobbied the Australian government for support. Prime Minister Billy Hughes responded generously; his offer included transport by rail from Sydney to Fremantle, by sea from Fremantle to Broome and Wallal, and return, with ten Australian naval personnel and a commander in attendance, as well as photographers, cinematographers, and one policeman.

In local language *wallal* means 'sweet water'. About fifty to a hundred Nyangumarta people lived there, some employed at Wallal Downs sheep station, with their elders living in a camp nearby. There was a post office and telegraph station, and a government-built well provided the precious groundwater of an abundant sandstone aquifer. There were no roads, only access by air or sea, with very high tides and heavy surf. The area is cyclone-prone. One struck in 1887, sinking more than forty pearling vessels and drowning hundreds of Malay and Aboriginal pearl divers. In 1908 a severe tropical cyclone again wrecked pearling ships, with loss of life, leaving Wallal Downs

23

station and post office in ruins. Newspapers reported bodies washed *ashore with every tide*. The *Beatrice* was wrecked in 1910, the *Ivydale* in 1916, the *Biddy* in 1919. But cyclone season was not due until November.

At a state luncheon in Perth on 17 August, the visiting scientists asked journalists to be patient. *The photographs we look for, the small angles we wish to detect, will not tell us their tale immediately*. Three days later they travelled on S.S. *Charon* to Broome, where they were joined by a team from India, and continued to Wallal on the 84-ton schooner *Gwendoline* towed by a small steamer. They arrived at sunrise on 30 August and anchored a few miles out. For their entire stay, the weather would be clear, with only gentle breezes to light winds.

Guided through the surf by Indigenous men and naval officers, the visitors were brought ashore in whaleboats. Everyone helped with unloading; suitcases, equipment and supplies, including bags of cement, were held high above the water, and reloaded onto carts drawn by a team of twenty-six donkeys. Photographers captured the scene, and it was filmed by Ernest 'Bud' Brandon-Cremer. His short documentary of the expedition now exists in two or more versions. Called *Astronomers and Aborigines*, it was renamed *The Sun Worshippers* and presented at London's Royal Albert Hall in May 1923. Now, to protect Indigenous cultural heritage, viewing of the original version is restricted.

The visitors would not have been aware of Aboriginal cosmology and the extent to which this knowledge – including laws against looking directly at solar eclipses – was woven into their lives and that some (but not all) Indigenous groups believed an eclipse was ominous. *While the specific details vary...many Aboriginal communities describe a dynamic between the Sun and Moon...one pursuing the other across the sky...occasionally meeting during an eclipse* (Hamacher and Norris).

Campbell, from the Lick Observatory, specialised in spectroscopy: he measured the spectrum of electromagnetic radiation. He was accompanied and assisted by his wife Elizabeth, astronomer Joseph Haines Moore, and galactic cluster expert Robert Trumpler, who had been in Tahiti to obtain comparison plates of stars in a place with nearly the same latitude as Wallal and with the same cameras to be used there. He had arrived early in Perth, to measure the Tahitian plates. Financed by W.H. Crocker, an American banker and philanthropist, they brought sophisticated equipment.

Astronomer Clarence Chant from the University of Toronto, his wife Jean, their daughter Elizabeth, and astronomer R.K. Young – all experienced eclipse expeditioners – made up the Canadian team. Astronomers John Evershed and Mary Acworth Evershed (he also a lepidopterist, she a botanist and Dante scholar) had come from Kodaikanal Observatory in India. New Zealand was represented by the scientist and government astronomer Charles Edward Adams and his wife Eleanor.

There was also a private party from England. James Hargreaves was president of the Chaldaean Society of observational astronomers and George Selwyn Clark-Maxwell (the Society's librarian) was a young optical engineer who would later study medicine and become a leading neurosurgeon; he was no relation to the Scottish physicist James Clerk Maxwell, one of Einstein's heroes. The other expeditioners regarded them as *English amateurs* from *somewhere near Cambridge*. But sponsored by the Royal Astronomical Society, and armed with a six-metre camera, smaller cameras, and a coelostat, they were (in a sense) Eddington's envoys, come to measure magnetic variations during totality, which they failed to do, owing to a smoky lamp. They needed the lamp (they later explained) to change the photographic plates, *because the darkness during totality [was] considerable*. But they made the most of their trip, Hargreaves continued to travel, and Maxwell found enough gold for an engagement ring (which he made himself) for his fiancée.

The Australian group camped near Wallal Downs station. They included Alexander Ross and Clive Nossiter of the Perth Observatory, W.E. Cooke of the Sydney Observatory, J.B.O. Hosking of the Melbourne Observatory, and J.J. Dwyer, a dapper photographer, flamboyantly moustached and always dressed in white. Responding to a rumour that this contingent would be subordinate to the Americans, *The West Australian* newspaper assured readers that our scientists had made their own plans to build their own bases and operate their own equipment, and to receive time signals from around the country and the world, and to establish Wallal's longitude, they would bring shortwave and longwave radios, to share with the visitors.

About a mile from the beach, among clumps of spinifex grass and stands of acacia trees, Nyangumarta men and the naval officers helped set up the camps – twelve sleeping tents, two mess tents, two store tents, a cook's galley – and four observing stations with concrete foundations and wooden towers and mechanized movement for telescopes and cameras. They contrived louvred canvas covers, to cool the sensitive equipment.

It's likely that the trees at Wallal were Yirrakulu (*Acacia eriopoda*, the narrowleaf or Broome wattle) and Wongai (*Acacia tumida*, or spear wattle). The Nyangumarta people used the protein-rich gum of both these kinds of acacia as food, and the wood to make spears and boomerangs; they made string from Wongai bark and flour for damper from roasted and ground seed pods.

A sign was attached to the large mess tent: Café Einstein. The naval officers provided the meals. Nyangumarta women fetched fresh water from the well, collected local fare like mussels, helped with cooking and serving; the visiting women helped wash the dishes. There was a hearty breakfast, lemonade at eleven, lunch, afternoon tea at four, dinner at seven. Elizabeth Campbell noted that *occasionally, as if by magic, an aviator would drop in for lunch.* The aviators were Norman Brearley and Charles Kingsford-Smith, bringing the mail on Saturdays and Mondays, years before Kingsford-Smith's famous flight across the Pacific. He took Brandon-Cremer on a flight to shoot aerial views of the camp.

For their leisure, they walked on the beach, swam, found shells. Trumpler in a sun hat, bare-chested, a Tahitian pareo wrapped around his waist. The Eversheds studied lizards, butterflies, moths and plants, including *Melaleuca glomerata* – desert honey myrtle – of which there are three specimens in the Perth Herbarium, said to have been collected in 1922 at Wallal Downs by a member of the Indian Eclipse Expedition; that collector must have been Mary Acworth Evershed. In one of the photos I see a deckchair in the shade of trees. They said at around forty degrees celsius the heat did not feel extreme. Flies and dust were a nuisance; because the topsoil was powdery, it was easily kicked up into a cloud, resembling (Campbell thought) *a comet's tail.*

Much work went into protecting equipment from dust and heat.

Each party had its own – as well as shared – interests and instruments. Photographic plates were vulnerable. The

Eversheds built three large concrete piers and a shelter for their cameras. To record a variety of eclipse phenomena, the Americans had spectographs, and different kinds of cameras with different-sized-lenses and focal lengths. Their Schaeberle camera needed a twelve-metre tower to be built, and an elaborate cover to protect and ventilate it. Its exact position was determined by the Australian scientists. The Americans also had two new Einstein cameras, called the 'Heavenly Twins', which needed their own supports and shelter; Trumpler assembled and tested them. Moore and Ross took charge of the spectrographs. The structures that held the cameras had to be strong and the fixtures had to be light-tight, with two layers of covering. For the eclipse, the alignment of cameras required absolute precision, as did the timing, with coordinates sent to Wallal telegraph station; at the camp Adams and his wife operated a wireless to determine accurate timing. There were many rehearsals.

It all depended on the weather. Campbell once said that eclipse astronomers feel their disappointment through clouds. On 21 September the newspapers announced a cloudless sky for Wallal, with a temperature of thirty-four degrees, some humidity, not much wind. To minimise dust on the morning of the eclipse, Nyangumarta men and women covered the ground around the site with heavier sand, dampened with water, and overlaid with wattle branches.

The eclipse began just after midday. Twenty minutes before totality, the sky's blue darkened and the landscape took on a purple hue. At twelve minutes, yellow light defined the horizon. At ten minutes, the sound of a gong meant the photographic plates had to be placed in position. Great visual clarity at four minutes, then white objects took on a range of blues. The Baily's

Beads phenomenon appeared just before totality, when the moon's outer circle sparkled *like the gems of a necklace* (*The Sydney Morning Herald*, 22.9.1922). The Nyangumarta people had retreated. At 1.40 p.m. the moon obscured the sun. Only its corona was visible, some said it was creamy white, other said it was flashing bright colours. *As soon as totality was reached, the long streamers of the corona came into view. These reached a length about four diameters of the sun. The centre disc was inky black...it was not positively dark, although one could not read print* (*The Northern Times*, 30.9.1922). Adams and his wife photographed the corona with an astrograph, which produced one of the defining images. Elizabeth Campbell managed the Lick exposures of the solar corona, a sight (she said) *wonderful beyond description*. The temperature dropped. Butcherbirds, songlarks, whistlers and wagtails and all the other birds were silent. Flies appeared paralysed. Sheep, cattle and horses grazed as they do at dusk. Totality lasted 5 minutes 15.5 seconds. Taking Beta Virginis as their guide, the expeditioners photographed the event with great accuracy, capturing the light of (an estimated) hundred stars, confident they would be able to measure the deflection of starlight in the sun's gravitational field.

Trumpler began immediately to develop the so-called Einstein plates in the darkroom tent, but stopped when weather conditions suddenly worsened, with more heat and humidity and strong winds spreading dust. This lasted for four days. They dismantled the camp. Again cases of equipment were transported on donkey trains to the beach where (a newspaper reported) visitors were camping *alfresco*, as fierce westerlies and heavy seas delayed their departure. The *Gwendoline* waited nearby for the transfer and the naval sloop *Geranium* was anchored further out. To everyone's horror, a whaleboat carrying an Einstein camera sank, but somehow the camera was saved. When *Gwendoline* had all on board on 26 September, *Geranium* towed her to Broome, arriving two days later. In a makeshift darkroom at Broome's radio station, they found they had about eighty star images. On the last evening in Broome they attended a corroboree. By mid-October they were in Fremantle, but not ready to make public announcements. A long stretch of careful work lay ahead of them. Einstein was awarded the Nobel Prize in Physics (for 1921) on 9 November 1922, not for his relativity theory but for services to theoretical physics and his discovery of the law of the photoelectric effect. He gave the prize money to Mileva Marić and their sons.

On their separate ways home the Wallal expeditioners would have heard the news that in Italy Mussolini was elected prime minister. Like *drums in the night* (to take the prescient title of Brecht's play, premiered in 1922) social change was deeply felt. Bonds were being broken with the past, there was a new consciousness of time. In his diary Thomas Mann wrote that in dealing with the problem of time, Einstein's theory *assumes a real urgency...that I anticipated in my conception of The Magic Mountain.* It's often noted that in the year Einstein received the Nobel Prize, James Joyce's (complete) *Ulysses*, T.S. Eliot's masterpiece *The Waste Land*, and Virginia Woolf's first experimental novel *Jacob's Room* were published. Reviewing *Ulysses*, Eliot called it *the most important expression which the present age has found.* Woolf thought Eliot was exaggerating. In *Fantasia of the Unconscious* (1922), D.H. Lawrence wrote (a little snidely), *We are all very pleased with Mr Einstein...the universe isn't a [Newtonian] spinning wheel, it is a cloud of bees flying and veering around.*

Einstein and Elsa were on a tour of Asia and the Middle East, fundraising for the Hebrew University which was being built in Jerusalem. In Ceylon (now Sri Lanka), unable to decline his hosts' arrangements, he was *bitterly ashamed* to ride in a rickshaw pulled by a fellow human being. Arriving in Singapore, they were met at Johnston's Pier by what seemed like the entire Jewish community. They stayed with the diamond merchant Alfred Montour and in the afternoon attended a reception at the palatial home of Sir Manasseh Meyer. Einstein missed the Nobel Prize ceremony on 10 December. Mid-December in Japan he heard impressive reports about the Wallal expedition. Two months later they spent twelve days in Palestine.

In April 1923 Campbell wrote to Einstein about the success of the eclipse observation in Australia. Campbell also sent a telegram to Dyson in the UK, announcing: THREE PAIRS AUSTRALIA TAHITI ECLIPSE PLATES MEASURED BY CAMPBELL TRUMPLER SIXTY TWO TO EIGHTY FOUR STARS...COMPLETELY CALCULATED...and advising that there was no need to repeat the Einstein Test at future eclipses. Campbell and Einstein corresponded but did not meet until 1931 at Mount Wilson Observatory near Los Angeles.

Many of the scientists at Wallal were veterans of previous eclipses and would go on to photograph others. In the summer of 1927, the Eversheds (now living in England) headed to Yorkshire.

Relativity theory was in the air, a mass phenomenon. The 1920s (the Einstein scholar Siegfried Grundmann contends) was a *relativistic decade*. And literary scholars have noted that poetry and books on astronomy were reviewed side by side in the literary journal *The Athenaeum*, where Virginia Woolf was a contributor. In 1926 Woolf wrote in her diary that she'd overheard discussions on Einstein, and (perhaps somewhat disingenuously) that they went beyond her own limits of understanding. She was writing *To the Lighthouse*, which (it might be said) comes with its own light source and gravitational field. It is imbued with notions of push and pull, nearness and distance, time and space, envisaging (for example) how an idea that seemed simple, *became in practice immediately complex; as the waves shape themselves symmetrically from the cliff top, but to the swimmer among them are divided by steep gulfs, and foaming crests.* The novel was published in May, and on 29 June 1927 at Bardon Fell in North Yorkshire, with a group that included her lover Vita Sackville-West, Woolf watched the total eclipse of the sun. *Very high, on a moor, boggy, heathery, with butts for grouse shooting...like the Haworth country...We could see by a gold spot where the sun was...Leonard kept looking at his watch...the sun... sailing at a great pace...we saw it crescent, burning red...red streamers...the colour was going out...the colours faded...the light sank and sank...We had fallen...The earth was dead...* Until the light came back. Throughout, she kept an eye on Vita.

A note: I use ellipsis to compress her diary's eclipse description; it is worth reading it in full. A second note: like Woolf, the writer Adalbert Stifter, describing the total eclipse on 8 July 1842 in Vienna, also likened the sinking light to *Ohnmacht*, a falling down, a swoon, not of people but of a giant body, the Earth. A third note: Mary Acworth Evershed (née Orr) grew up in Cornwall, within view of the Godrevy lighthouse, which was the inspiration for the central image of Woolf's novel. Both Mary and Virginia signed the lighthouse visitors' book.

Woolf's next book *Orlando: A Biography* was already taking

shape. In it she wants *sapphism...to be suggested* and intends it to be a portrait of Vita, *a biography beginning in the year 1500 & continuing to the present day.* Clearly, her Yorkshire experience was fresh in her mind. When Orlando is betrayed in love, he quotes Shakespeare's Othello (after he had smothered Desdemona) conjuring an image of a *huge eclipse of sun and moon,* foreshadowing his (Orlando's) own transition from man to woman. And a note here too: Woolf was a great admirer of the work of Emily Brontë, whose poetry she placed even higher than her novel. At the eclipse in Yorkshire – Haworth country, Haworth sky – Woolf would have recalled 'Stars', one of Brontë's most exhilarating love poems, in which the poet enacts a passionate drama of dark and light, night and day.

Writing *Orlando,* Woolf threw it all into the ring: time, place, gender, genre, language. She wanted e*verything...tumbled in pell mell,* from large vistas and faraway places to *little ideas and tiny stories* (*Diary, 1925–30*). And although she intended it to end with three dots...elliptically...the published version ends with its own publication date, *midnight, Thursday, the eleventh of October, Nineteen Hundred and Twenty-Eight.* A novel, it bows coquettishly to biographical convention by including an index.

As if in conversation with Einstein, modernist writers and artists experimented with new aesthetics. One reviewer wrote, *for lack of a better term, we might describe [Orlando] as an application of the Einstein theory of relativity* (*NYT* 21.10.1928).

Einstein was in great demand, his life was hectic. In the summer of 1927 he spent time with his son Eduard in Zuoz, a village in the Swiss Alps. He tells his other son that rather than mountain climbing they had been discussing Nietzsche, but plan to *hike to Maloja and then over the Septimer Pass. Then we go on to Berlin via Zürich. Before all that I was in Geneva.* A few months later he was at the fifth Solvay Conference in Brussels, to discuss electrons, photons and quantum theory with Niels Bohr, Max Born, Marie Curie, Werner Heisenberg, and Max Planck, among others.

Biographers have traced midlife changes in Einstein's scientific path, from revolutionary to conservative. Unconvinced by theories of randomness, chance and probability, he would not abandon the idea of causality and kept searching for a unified field to integrate electricity, magnetism, gravity and quantum mechanics. There are stories of his intense discussions about this with his friend, the physicist and philosopher Niels Bohr, on a tram in Copenhagen, continuously missing their stop and going back and forth on the same route, their friendship engendering (privately and publicly) great intellectual debate, about what can and can't be known, or observed, in quantum mechanics, with Einstein unable to accept the idea of coincidence.

In March 1928 he was invited to lecture in Davos and had a heart attack while taking a short break nearby in Zuoz, followed by months of illness. That year he spent his most memorable Baltic holiday in Scharbeutz, a village thirty kilometres northwest of Lübeck. He went there to recover his health, but also to escape the rounds of doctors. Arriving in early July to stay in Villa Michahelles, a large airy house on a rise that overlooked the sea, his entourage consisted of his wife Elsa, her daughter Margot, his friend Toni Mendel, his daughter-in-law Frieda, and Helen Dukas, the secretary he'd recently appointed to lighten his workload. His sister Maja arrived later, other family members and friends – and doctors – dropped in for shorter visits.

Writing to Eduard, Einstein explained he could not visit the family in Switzerland, as promised, because his heart condition had deteriorated, he had been in bed for weeks, and was advised against high altitudes. Scharbeutz was good for him; he sat under the trees, with a view to the sea, his favourite kind of landscape. Sad only because he was still too weak to go sailing. He was *condemned to a life of leisure, beneath splendid beech trees on the Baltic*, he tells another of his correspondents.

The trees surrounding the villa, and other groves in the region, were remnants of ancient expanses of beech or mixed forest that grew along the southern Baltic coastline from Sweden, Denmark, Germany, Poland, to East Prussia. Einstein and Toni shared a love of reading. Now they read Proust and Freud. He had met Freud and admired him but thought he lacked a spiritual dimension and showed a certain deafness *to the music of the spheres*. Whether something had *musicality* or not, was also how he judged scientific theories and discoveries. In the beech trees' play of light and shade he read Schopenhauer, Plato, and *Spinoza with great pleasure*. Rabelais's *Gargantua* made him laugh. Most likely there was always a copy of *Don Quixote* to hand. And he enjoyed the attention of all the women, he called them his *harem*.

One day in early September the Warburgs arrived. Art historian Aby Warburg was fascinated by ellipses – in science and culture – and came to discuss Johannes Kepler with Einstein, specifically Kepler's discovery that the orbit of Mars around the sun was not circular but elliptical. Warburg's magnificent new research library in Hamburg featured an elliptical reading room because (it's been suggested) circles make you sleepy while ellipses keep you alert. To illustrate his ideas, Warburg had brought his *Bilderatlas Mnemosyne*, an atlas of art and memory, to show Einstein. A year later Warburg died of a heart attack.

Einstein's health was improving. He told a friend: *The inner thump-thump has settled down, but a real schlemiel has remained behind...[with] nothing of proud splendour apart from a healthy sense of humour.* He wrote to Hans Albert: *Here I look down on the Bay of Lübeck, a splendid landscape, but damn! I can't sail around it.* And to Eduard, that he found the coastal landscape so beautiful, *I'm already dreading my departure.* He urged him to join them. *Warm regards from your Papa.* Not being able to go sailing was an agony, and briefly, in late September, he broke free. According to Elsa he disappeared and completely exhausted himself by sitting for hours *in a rocking boat in a strong wind [with] a long walk back from the jetty.* Uphill to the Villa Michahelles. She ordered three days of bed rest to recover. Einstein joked that if he died, his two months of *humble existence in nature* were like a *preparation for paradise.* But Baltic seasons change abruptly. The group left when the sea turned *into a frozen lake.* The Villa Michahelles was demolished in 1969. It was replaced by a block of holiday apartments, bearing a plaque to say Einstein stayed there in 1928. The surrounding beech forest is gone.

For his fiftieth birthday, his friends gave him a sailboat called *Tümmler* (porpoise; though in Yiddish *tumler* is a prankster), he received congratulations from around the world, and from the German government (after the embarrassment of not having a present) the promise of a lake house. That promise came with complications, and at his own cost Einstein had a house designed by Konrad Wachsmann and built on the Schwielowsee at Caputh near Potsdam. He made sure there was no telephone.

It became his refuge for the next three summers. A decade later he would help Wachsmann emigrate to America.

When he met Charlie Chaplin in 1931, they joked about their popularity, that it was an odd phenomenon, since (in his films) Chaplin doesn't speak, and (in his lectures) Einstein is difficult to understand. His friends urged him to protest more loudly against the rise of fascism, which he did.

He wrote to Freud. *You have shown with irresistible lucidity how inseparably the aggressive and destructive forces are bound up in the human psyche with those of love and the lust for life.* He situates Freud with other *moral and spiritual leaders* (Jesus, Goethe, Kant) who argued against war, but whose words were ineffective. He wonders if an international organisation of honest and concerned intellectuals could not become a new force against the rising dangers of politics. To form such an association *seems to me nothing less than an imperative duty!*

He asked Freud the question which still plagues us. *Is there any way of delivering mankind from the menace of war?* An issue, he says, that *has come to mean a matter of life and death for Civilization as we know it.* Personally, he confessed, he had *no insight into the dark places of human will and feeling.* Freud thought this problem lies *on the borderland of the knowable*, and although his answer was expansive, it lacked vigour. Their exchange shows Einstein as optimist (looking for an end to war), Freud as pessimist (claiming the inevitability of war).

In 1932 Einstein met with two more likeminded friends, Käthe Kollwitz and Heinrich Mann, to organise the Urgent Call for Unity to stop the National Socialists from gaining ground at the Reichstag election in July. *Let us ensure that no sloth of nature or cowardice of heart allow us to sink into barbarism!* Signed by over thirty prominent citizens, including the economist Franz Oppenheimer (unrelated to J. Robert Oppenheimer), playwright Ernst Toller, and children's book author Erich Kästner, it was published in a socialist newspaper and appeared on posters across Berlin. Since Kollwitz's eighteen-year-old son Peter was killed in action in Flanders in October 1914, she had been a pacifist and the depiction of grief had become her life's work. After her meeting with Einstein, she and her husband travelled to Belgium for the unveiling of her 'Grieving Parents' sculptures in the cemetery where their son was buried.

The Einsteins left Germany on 10 December 1932 and never returned.

The Urgent Call – and its follow-up in early 1933 – as with all other efforts to stop this flow of evil, were unsuccessful. Hitler came to power in 1933. Einstein renounced his German citizenship and started to question the usefulness of his belief in pacifism. By April, German Jews were being dismissed from public institutions. Human tragedy on an unimaginable scale lay ahead. Like others who managed to flee, Einstein was now a refugee. He was also in danger. He visited his family in Switzerland and went to Belgium and England, where he was taken into hiding in the Norfolk countryside, with armed protection. Before leaving Britain he spoke at an event to raise funds for refugees. No longer German, he now described himself as *a good European*. He and Elsa arrived in New York on 17 October 1933. Taking up a position at Princeton, and asked what he needed, he requested a desk, chair, paper, pencils and a large wastepaper basket *so I can throw away all my mistakes*. In Hamburg, Warburg's precious library of sixty thousand books was saved from desecration by being moved to London.

When Einstein read Joseph Roth's *Job* – about exile – in early 1935, he called it a *consoling* book by a real mensch and a great writer. Later that year, he and Thomas Mann were awarded honorary doctorates at Harvard; in Mann's words, a *tremendous acclamation for Einstein and me*. The citation called Einstein *a great revolutionist of theoretical physics*.

On his voyage to New York – *westward across the ocean's curve...the absolute void before us* – Thomas Mann had been re-reading *Don Quixote* and had written an essay about that experience, which reflects on the vastness of time and space, on our childlike cosmological wonder and naïvety, and (regarding that kind of wonder) *Albert Einstein's bright round eyes, like a child's*. His son Klaus Mann saw Einstein differently, describing his *wily piercing glance*.

People like to read and assign meaning to Einstein's face, habits, quirks. In her essay on Lotte Jacobi's photographs, Gretchen Gasterland-Gustafsson selects an image in which Einstein *looks comfortable, casual, and somewhat fragile*. Jacobi – a fellow refugee and trusted friend – had photographed him for many years, in different situations and moods. This photo belonged to a series taken at his home in Princeton in 1938. He is holding a pen above some paper, the folds of his leather jacket catch *ambient light from an unseen window*, on his face a distant gaze. A thinker, Gustafsson observes, in the act of thinking.

After Elsa Einstein's death in December 1936, his household consisted of his sister, his stepdaughter Margot, and personal assistant Helen Dukas, a cat, a dog who bit the mailman, and a parrot; he liked macaroni for lunch; liked walking alone, though he sometimes had to ask for directions. *Excuse me, I'm Albert Einstein and...* His son Hans Albert and family came to America.

His son Eduard was a patient at Burghölzli, the University of Zürich's psychiatric clinic.

Proudly Jewish and respectful of Zionism, he would always remain uneasy about the idea of Jewish nationalism. In April 1938 in New York, in a speech to the National Labor Committee for Palestine, he said, *I should much rather see agreement with the Arabs on the basis of living together in peace than the creation of a Jewish state...a Jewish state with borders, an army, a measure of temporal power no matter how modest... I am afraid of the inner damage Judaism will sustain.*

In August 1939 Einstein wrote to President Roosevelt, warning that the Germans were working on an atomic bomb. *Sir...the element of uranium may be turned into a new and important source of energy in the immediate future. Certain aspects of the situation...seem to call for watchfulness and if necessary, quick action.* In 1940 he became an American citizen. Regarded as a safety risk, he was excluded from the Manhattan Project to develop an atomic bomb.

In 1941 he persuaded one of his oldest friends, the psychiatrist Otto Juliusburger and his family to leave Germany, paid for their travel expenses, and once they were settled in New York, they frequently visited each other. The following year Einstein, aged in his sixties, wrote to Juliusburger, in his seventies, to say that they'll never grow old *because we never cease to stand like curious children before the great mystery into which we were born.*

Virginia Woolf was deeply disturbed by the devastation of war and the threat of German invasion; she committed suicide in 1941. On 3 May 1945, four months before the end of World War II, the SS *Thielbek* and SS *Cap Arcona* were sunk during Allied bombings in the Bay of Lübeck. Communication between the

British commanders and the pilots had failed, and the pilots did not know those ships were carrying over 4,500 internees from Neuengamme concentration camp. 4,000 died. For years their bodies washed onto the beaches; they were buried in mass graves. A memorial cemetery in Scharbeutz marks one of those sites. On 6 August 1945 the atom bomb was dropped on Hiroshima, three days later a second bomb was dropped on Nagasaki. Einstein was shocked and saddened. While some held him responsible for the tragic event, he steadfastly continued to campaign for world peace and nuclear arms control. A speech he presented on December 1945 at the Astor in New York, called 'The war is won, but the peace is not', warns that *the picture of our postwar world is not bright.*

From 1952 to 1956 the British conducted three nuclear tests on the Montebello Islands about 120 kilometres off the Western Australian coast near Wallal. Information about the tests is still classified and tourists are warned to limit site visits to one hour. It's known that oceanic currents carry radioactive sediment far from its source.

On the public stage and especially in his later years, Einstein was often regarded as a 'character'. In 1947 he was portrayed by actor and fellow refugee Ludwig Stössel in a film about the atom bomb, *The Beginning or the End*. Stössel was one of the few actors able to turn a German accent into an asset for funny foreigner roles, such as Herr Leuchtag in *Casablanca*, who summed up the awkwardness of refugees when he asks Frau Leuchtag what time it is: *Liebchen...Sweetnessheart. What watch?* (She) *Ten watch.* (He) *Such watch.* Though endearingly accented, Einstein's English was very good. He was confident enough to be witty. He would readily explain the theory of relativity to anyone who asked, adding that it is *a somewhat unfamiliar conception for the average mind.*

Einstein headed The Emergency Committee of Atomic Scientists. They met in April 1948 to discuss the collapse of atomic negotiations at the United Nations. *They talked in calm tones, but the pictures they conjured were lethal. They painted a nightmare world... Prof. Einstein sat behind the table in his characteristic informal attire, rough blue sweater, open collar and gray trousers.* To prevent the end of human civilisation, he argued, world federation is the world's only hope, but partial world government would be a start in the right direction (Leon Edel, *PM*, 12.4.1948).

Mileva Marić died in 1948. Maja Winteler (Einstein) died in 1951. That year Einstein and others protested against German rearmament. In 1952 he declined an offer to become president of Israel. In physics, he regretted that relativity, uncertainty and incompleteness seemed irreconcilable, and continued searching for a unified field theory. Towards the end of his life he chose two books of travel, Goethe's *Wilhelm Meisters Wanderjahre* and *Don Quixote*, to read aloud. His friend the photographer Philippe Halsman has pointed out that Einstein was determined – and it took him many months – to read both books from beginning to end, and that he never lost his sense of humour, despite being in great pain.

In the private collection of the Einstein Library at the Einstein Papers Project – alongside Humboldt, Kant, Lessing, Mach, Nietzsche, Russell, Schopenhauer, Tolstoy, and others – there are six Cervantes-related items, including an early German edition, *Leben und Thaten des scharfsinnigen Edlen Don Quixote von la Mancha*, translated by the Romantic poet Ludwig Tieck in 1799–1801, and (perhaps this was the last book he read) Peter

Schunck's late nineteenth-century translation, *Don Kichote: Ein drolliges Heldengedicht*. Einstein died at Princeton Hospital on 18 April 1955.

On 17 March 1966 in *The New York Review of Books*, J. Robert Oppenheimer praised Einstein profusely and exonerated him from blame for *these miserable bombs...the supreme violence of these atomic weapons*, emphasising they were never Einstein's intention and were developed *by accident* by others. Indeed, by Oppenheimer himself. But his hyperbole – that Einstein was the greatest physicist and natural philosopher of our time, *the friendliest of men*, of *luminous* intelligence – camouflaged another set of views. Oppenheimer thought Einstein's last twenty-five years were a failure, that he was a loner who lacked deeper human affections and scientific cooperation, his early papers (while *paralysingly beautiful*) were full of errors, he was not a good violinist, he was unsophisticated, lacked *background*, and (unlike Gandhi) lacked leadership. Two months later the *NYRB* printed Philippe Halsman's response to what he called Oppenheimer's *beautifully phrased and delicate venom*. It had distressed him because it was untrue. Einstein was *a human being full of empathy and warmth, a man of rare selflessness and touching modesty, always ready to oppose injustice, to fight for an underdog, or to help a victim*, he knew this firsthand, because Einstein had saved his life by helping him leave Germany.

Some science writers still ask if Eddington or Dyson 'cooked' the data by 'averaging' the Príncipe and Sobral measurements to match Einstein's prediction. To add to that mystery, Eddington's photographic plates from Príncipe, the crown jewels of twentieth-century experimental science, on which everything hinged in 1919, have disappeared, nobody knows when or how, possibly in the 1970s when they were removed from the archive to be remeasured. Many of Eddington's personal papers have also disappeared, destroyed by himself, his sister, and (it's thought) by the astrophysicist F.J.M. 'Chubby' Stratton during an overly efficient clean-up of the Cambridge Observatory. In their paper 'The 1919 eclipse results that verified General Relativity and their later detractors: a story retold', Professor Gerard Gilmore and Dr Gudrun Tausch-Pebody have addressed the complexities of this controversy.

In the early 1980s Jeffrey Crelinsten pointed out that Einstein's biographies focused on the British eclipse expeditions and ignored other attempts to test relativity. Forty years later, this is still the case. Scholars have written papers on Wallal – arguably the most successful of all the expeditions – but it is rarely (if ever?) mentioned by Einstein's recent biographers. I asked Walter Isaacson why he did not include the Wallal expedition in his book; he said he could not remember the reason.

In an interview, Leon Edel (who wrote a five-volume biography of Henry James) said all his work has been *a search for form, really experiments in form*. The interviewer asks, *And did you originally plan that this would be a five-volume work?* To which Edel answers enthusiastically, *Oh no. I planned a single volume, in three parts… I invented my form as I went along…my volumes grew longer, the second volume became two volumes.*

Edel's is the readerly way of writing biography. And as biographical experiments continue to pitch form – organic form – against formula, there's a new generation of biographers in the wings, for whom excursions to Wallal, Yorkshire, Scharbeutz, and other places, are part of our collective – 'unified field' – understanding of Einstein's life and times.

Interviewer: *Is biography really an art or is it, in fact, a structural piecing together of fragments – a form of carpentry?*

Edel: *There is carpentry involved, but what I was doing was finding a form to suit my materials as I went along, having from the first given myself a large design... All this required what I like to call the biographical imagination, the imagination of form.*

Sources

Brandon-Cremer, Ernest, *The Sun Worshipers*, documentary, https://aso.gov.au/titles/documentaries/sun-worshippers/clip1/.

Campbell, W.W., 'The Total Eclipse of the Sun, September 21, 1922', lecture, *Astronomical Society of the Pacific*, Vol. 35, No. 203, 1923.

Chant, C. A., 'The Eclipse Camp at Wallal', *The Journal of the Royal Astronomical Society of Canada*, Vol. 17, No. 1, 1923.

Crelinsten, Jeffery, 'William Wallace Campbell and the "Einstein Problem": An Observational Astronomer confronts the Theory of Relativity', *Historical Studies in the Physical Sciences*, Vol. 14, No. 1, 1983; *Einstein's Jury: The Race to Test Relativity*, Princeton University Press, 2006.

Edel, Leon, 'The Art of Biography No.1', interviewed by Jeanne McCullough, *The Paris Review*, Issue 98, 1985; *Writing Lives: Principia Biographica*, W. W. Norton, 1984.

Debord, Guy, 'Theory of the Dérive', *Les Lèvres Nues 9*, trans. Ken Knabb, 1956.

Eddington, A. S, Papers of Sir Arthur Eddington, correspondence 1899–1943, Trinity College Library, Cambridge.

Einstein, Albert, *Relativity: The Special and The General Theory*, Methuen, 1920; 'The War Is Won but the Peace Is Not' speech, https://www.youtube.com/watch?v=n9DKJKJuZJI; The Collected Papers of Albert Einstein, https://einsteinpapers.press.princeton.edu/.

Fölsing, Albrecht, *Albert Einstein: Eine Biographie*, Suhrkamp, 1993.

Freud-Einstein correspondence, https://www.public.asu.edu/~jmlynch/273/documents/FreudEinstein.pdf.

Gasterland-Gustafsson, Gretchen, 'A Portrait of Albert Einstein', https://smarthistory.org/lotte-jacobi-albert-einstein/.

Gilmore, Gerard and Tausch-Pebody, Gudrun, 'The 1919 Eclipse Results that verified General Relativity and their later detractors: a story retold', *The Royal Society Journal of the History of Science*, 2021, https://royalsocietypublishing.org/doi/full/10.1098/rsnr.2020.0040.

Goyder, Roma (ed), *Hayseed to Harvest: Memories of Katherine Cox and Hayes Court School*, Fletcher & Fletcher, 1985.

Grundmann, Siegfried, *The Einstein Dossiers: Science and Politics*, Springer, 2005.

Halsman, Philippe, 'Einstein', *The New York Review of Books*, 26 Mary, 1966.

Hamacher, Duane .W. and Norris, Ray P., 'Eclipses in Australian Aboriginal Astronomy', *Journal of Astronomical History and Heritage*, Vol. 14 No. 2, 2011.

Isaacson, Walter, *Einstein: His Life and Universe*, Simon & Schuster, 2007.

Kennefick, Daniel, *No Shadow of a Doubt: The 1919 Eclipse That Confirmed Einstein's Theory of Relativity*, Princeton University Press, 2019.

Lomb, Nick and Stevenson, Toner, *Eclipse Chasers*, CSIRO Publishing, 2023.

Manguel, Alberto, *A History of Reading*, HarperCollins, 1996.

Miller, Arthur I., *Empire of the Stars: Obsession, Friendship, and Betrayal in the Quest for Black Holes*, Mariner, 2005.

Neffe, Jürgen, *Einstein: Eine Biographie*, Rowohlt, 2005.

Oppenheimer, Robert, 'On Albert Einstein', *The New York Review of Books*, 17 March 1966.

Stanley, Matthew, *Einstein's War*, Dutton, 2019.

Woolf, Virginia, *To the Lighthouse*, Hogarth Press, 1927; *Orlando*, Hogarth Press, 1928; *The Death of the Moth*, Hogarth Press, 1930; *The Common Reader: Second Series*, Hogarth Press, 1932; *The Diary of Virginia Woolf*, Vol 3.: 1925–30, Penguin Classics, 1982.

Young, R.K., 'The Canadian Eclipse Expedition', *The Journal of the Royal Astronomical Society of Canada*, Vol. 17, 1923.

I was four in 1954 when we holidayed on the northernmost tip of Denmark, where the North Sea meets the Baltic, and where (I was told later) I missed a near-total eclipse of the sun because I was having a nap.

With thanks to Bill Barton FRAS, Marnee Gamble, Professor Gretchen Gasterland-Gustafsson, Professor Gerard Gilmore, Michael Gregg, Professor Walter Isaacson, Professor Daniel Kennefick, Professor Stephen van Leeuwen, Bruce Maslin AM, Ilona Richter, Ze'ev Rosenkranz, Professor Matthew Stanley, Dr Gudrun Tausch-Pebody, Jean Wilson.

SUNEETA PERES DA COSTA
THREE POEMS

Suneeta Peres da Costa lives on unceded Gadigal land. Her most recent book, *Saudade*, focuses on the legacies of Portuguese colonialism and the Goan diaspora in pre-Independence Angola. It was shortlisted for the 2019 Prime Minister's Literary Awards, the 2020 Adelaide Festival Awards for Literature, and was a finalist in the 2020 Tournament of Books. Her literary honours include a Fulbright Scholarship, the Australia Council for the Arts BR Whiting Studio Residency, Rome, and an Asialink Arts Creative Exchange to North India. Her first collection of poetry, *The Prodigal*, will be published by Giramondo in 2024.

What He Did and Didn't Eat

Not – olives. Pumpkin but not zucchini; carrots but not peas.
Eggs, scrambled, poached or baked but never, ever raw. So too
mushrooms. Hard cheese but oh, no, not soft cheese (whether
crème fraiche or mascarpone), nor washed rind cheese, nor
any category of yoghurt. Surprisingly neither raspberries,
nor blueberries, nor for that matter tropical fruits; star fruit,
mangosteen and lychees – totally out of the question!

The Doctor of Philosophy

He had been working on the same project, a study of the
heliotropic properties of a certain kind of rare wildflower,
found only in the foothills of the Pennine Alps, for longer
than he could remember. His days were spent predictably –
confined to the laboratory, squinting through the artificial
light of the microscope or crushing seed to prepare petri
specimens. Late into the night he could also be found,
hunched over a rickety desk in his bedroom, poring over
textbooks or writing up notes from his lab experiments.
He shared a cramped apartment with two fellow students
(one, a hirsute astrophysicist, who engaged in terminal
procrastination perfecting Bach's Cello Suites; the other,
a German literature major, as fixated with the death of
Ingeborg Bachmann as the state of domestic hygiene, and who
registered his distress by way of hysterical, corrective notes he
scattered here and there). If he himself had any time at all to
spare for leisure, he would take long hikes into the mountains.
He would feel an urge to go even though snow was falling and
the bite of winter had settled in. He had no reason to analyse
then, when there was hardly any sunlight nor likelihood of
sighting gentians nor black vanilla orchids; then, when there
was least reason for it – or shall we say, evidence? – why he
should feel the singular, almost prophetic, importance of his
scholarly enterprise.

The Abandoned Panettone

How difficult it might be to abandoned and alone, at Easter, at Roma Trastevere Station, watching trains arriving and leaving without you to all sorts of exciting destinations; knowing everyone else was on their way up to the mountains, or off to the seaside; to visit with friends and family; to partake of festive wine and cured olives and fattened, delicately spiced, young lamb. To know that children were running delighted, their laughter and footsteps echoing through hallways and across gardens, as they searched for hidden chocolate. To, in short, be a panettone without a ticket, forgotten, left behind. Worse, to unwittingly draw attention to yourself, to be unjustly suspected and surrounded by the carabinieri, poked and prodded until your gold ribbon came completely undone, and your lovely firm packaging was destroyed by the impact of a random baton!

SARA MESA
UN AMOR

Translated from the Spanish by Katie Whittemore

Sara Mesa is the author of ten works
of fiction, including *Scar* (winner of
the Ojo Critico Prize), *Four by Four*
(a finalist for the Herralde Prize), *An
Invisible Fire* (winner of the Premio
Málaga de Novela), and *Cara de Pan*.
Her books have been translated into
more than ten different languages,
and widely praised for their concise,
sharp style. Her novel, *Un Amor*, from
which this story is drawn, will shortly
be published in English.

Katie Whittemore translates from
the Spanish. Her work has appeared
in *Two Lines, The Los Angeles Review,
The Brooklyn Rail, InTranslation* and
elsewhere. Current projects include
novels by Spanish authors Sara Mesa,
Javier Serena, Aliocha Coll, Aroa
Moreno Durán, Nuria Labari, Katixa
Agirre and Juan Gómez Bárcena.

THE HOUSE IN LA ESCAPA is a squat structure, single-storey, with windows practically level with the ground and one bedroom with two single beds. Nat wanted the landlord to take away one of the beds – she won't need it – so she could set up a desk instead. She'd be fine with a plain board with four legs. She considers calling him but keeps putting it off. When she does see him – she'll have to see him sooner or later – she will ask. Or hint. For the time being, she'll work without a desk, making do with the only table, which she moves against the wall because the house is gloomy and damp, even during the day. The kitchen – little more than a countertop and hob – is so grim that she has to turn on the overhead light just to make a cup of coffee. Outside is different. Starting at daybreak, the sun beats down on the land, and working in the yard, even first thing in the morning, is exhausting. She tries hoeing rows to plant peppers, tomatoes, carrots, whatever grows fast and easily. She read about doing it. She's even seen a few videos that explain the process step by step, but once she's in the dirt, she's incapable of putting any of it into practice. She'll have to get over her embarrassment and ask somebody.

She sits down in the evening to translate for an hour or two. She can never quite concentrate. Maybe she requires an adaptation period, she tells herself, no need to obsess yet. To clear her head, she takes walks around the surrounding area. No matter how much she calls him, Sieso, the stray dog that has been scratching around in the dirt, refuses to accompany her, and so she goes alone, listening to music on her earphones. When she sees someone else approaching, she speeds up, even jogs a bit. She prefers to go unnoticed, not be forced to introduce herself or chat, even if that means pretending to exercise.

Cork oaks, holm oaks, and olive trees stud the drought-ridden terrain. The rockrose, sticky and unassuming, is the only flower to dot the land. The monotony of the fields is broken up only by the mass of El Glauco, a low mountain of bush and shrub that looks like it's been sketched in charcoal on a naked sky. On El Glauco, it is said, there are still foxes and wild boar, though the hunters who go up only come back with strings of quail and rabbit on their belts. It's a spooky mountain, Nat thinks, quickly dismissing the thought. Why spooky? Glauco is an ugly name, for sure; she supposes it must come from its pale, wan colour. The word *glauco* reminds her of a diseased eye, with conjunctivitis, or elderly eyes, glassy and red, almost tarnished. She realises she's letting herself be influenced by the meaning of *glaucoma*. Coincidentally, the word *glauco* has appeared in the book she is attempting to translate, as an adjective attributed to the main character, the fearsome father who at a certain point unleashes an injurious imprecation at one of his sons, while he, according to the text, fixes him with a glaucous gaze. At first, Nat thought of an eye infection, but later understood that a glaucous gaze is simply an empty, inexpressive look, the kind in which the pupil appears dead, almost opaque. What, then, is the correct meaning? *Light green, blueish green, sickly, dim, distant?* She will have to orient the rest of the paragraph around the term she chooses. Opting for a literal translation without understanding the genuine spirit of the sentence would be like cheating.

No matter how much she cleans, everything is dirty. She sweeps and sweeps but the dust comes in through the cracks and accumulates in the corners. If she at least had a fan for sleeping, she thinks, she could close the windows and everything would be more comfortable. She would wake up rested and with more energy to clean, translate, and work in the garden – or, plan for the garden, more like it. Asking the landlord for a fan doesn't even cross her mind.

She decides to go to Petacas to buy one. While she's at it, she thinks, she might as well get some tools. A hoe, buckets, a shovel, pruning shears, sieve, and a few other things. She can always figure out the exact names of what she needs.

She knows nothing about tools.

She is surprised by the activity in Petacas. It takes her a while to find parking; the layout of the roads is so chaotic and the signage so contradictory that once you enter the town, an unexpected detour can easily take you right out of it again. The houses are modest, façades worse for wear and mostly plain, but there are brick buildings too, up to six storeys tall, distributed arbitrarily here and there. The businesses are clustered around the main square; the town hall – an ostentatious building with large eaves and stained-glass windows – is surrounded by small bars and Chinese-owned bazaars. Nat buys a fan at one of them. Then she wanders in search of a hardware store, reluctant to ask for directions. She is struck by the neglected appearance of the women, who go around with dishevelled hair wearing sandals. Lots of the men – even the old ones – are wearing singlets. There are just a few children, and they're unsupervised, licking popsicles, scampering, rolling on the ground. The people – men, women, kids – all loud and sloppy, look strangely alike. Inbreeding, Nat thinks. Her landlord fits in perfectly.

She is worried about running into him, but it's Píter, the one they call 'the hippie', not the landlord, whom she meets in the hardware store. She is happy to see him: someone friendly, someone finally smiling at her, coming over, what are you doing here, he asks. Nat shows him the box with the fan and he scowls. Why didn't she ask the landlord? It's his responsibility to keep the property in habitable condition. Not air conditioning, of course, but a fan at least.

'Or you could have asked me. That's what neighbours are for.'

Nat looks for an excuse. She's happy to buy one, she says. When she leaves La Escapa, she'll take it with her. He looks at her sideways, pretending not to believe her.

'And what did you come here to buy? Tools to fix everything he left broken?' Nat shakes her head.

'No. Stuff for the garden.' 'You're going to plant a garden?'

'Well, just something basic... Peppers and eggplants, I guess they're easy. I at least want to try.'

Píter takes her by the arm, steps in closer. 'Don't buy anything,' he whispers.

He tells her that he can lend her all the tools she needs. He says, too, that she might as well forget the idea of a garden. Nothing's grown on her land in years; the soil is totally depleted; it would take days and days of hard work to get it into shape. If she insists – Nat hangs on that word, *insists* – he could lend her a hand, but he absolutely advises against it. Although he speaks smoothly, Píter's voice contains indisputable certainty, an expert's confidence. Nat nods, waits for him to finish his shopping. Cables, adaptors, screws, a pair of pliers: all very professional, very specific, nothing at all like the cloudiness she moves in.

Outside, Píter walks next to her at a sportive pace, straight but flexible. His way of moving is so elegant, so different from the people around them, that Nat is proud to be walking alongside him, the kind of pride associated with legitimacy. When he points out the windows at the town hall, the spell is broken.

'Pretty, aren't they? I made them myself.'

The windows clash terribly with the building's exposed brick, but she is all praise: they suit it perfectly, she says. Píter looks at her appreciatively. Precisely, he says, that's what he seeks, that his work be appropriate to its context.

'Petacas isn't the prettiest place in the world, but, to the extent they can, people should work to make their surroundings more beautiful, don't you think?'

'So, you're a...' Nat doesn't know what you call a person who makes stained-glass windows. 'A glazier? Yes. Well, more than a glazier. You could say I'm a glass and colour artisan. Like, I don't just cover windows.'

'Of course.' Nat smiles.

They have a beer in one of the bars on the square. The beer is ice-cold and goes down easy. Píter observes her closely – too closely, she thinks – but his eyes are sweet and that softens her discomfort. The conversation returns to the landlord – that cheeky bastard, he repeats – the tools and her barren plot. He insists on lending her what she needs. Just a matter of tidying the yard, clearing it for a table and some lawn chairs, then planting a few oleander and yucca, or some succulents suitable for the harsh climate. There's a huge nursery near Petacas, very cheap. If she wants, they can go together someday. Her plans for a vegetable garden appear to be scrapped. She doesn't even mention them again.

She devotes the next few days to the exterior part of the house. She rises early to avoid the heat, but even so, she sweats nonstop, and a grubby feeling stays with her all day. She scrubs the porch, scrapes, sands, and stains the pergola's wood floor and beams, prunes the withered branches that run rampant, pulls weeds, removes bag after bag of rubbish – papers, dry leaves, metal, plastic, empty cans, more broken branches. The final result is basically a wide expanse of cracked dirt. If the house were hers, she thinks, she would put in a lawn, and maybe the oleanders Píter recommended, they would make a natural fence to shelter her from prying eyes, but that's dumb, the house isn't hers, she's not going through all that effort for nothing.

One morning, the gypsy woman from the village outskirts pokes her head in the gate and asks if Nat wants any flowerpots.

'I got tons,' she says.

She sells Nat a whole bunch for cheap. They're all old, but Nat isn't bothered by the chips on the ceramic pots or the mildew on the clay ones. There are two huge urns as well, and once they're scrubbed clean, they strike her as lovely. Since they're quite heavy, the gypsy's husband helps her carry them home, accompanied by two of their three sons. Nat likes that family. They're rowdy and good-natured. The kids pet Sieso and, for the first time, she sees the dog wag his tail and turn in a circle with an instinct to play.

'Just pick some sprouts when you're out and about and you'll have the garden ready in no time,' the gypsy husband says as he's leaving. 'You don't need the nursery or nothing.'

It's true. Nat picks plants from nearby houses, many of them empty, branches that poke through the fences around the properties and whose loss doesn't pose any problem to the owners. Nevertheless, Píter is annoyed when he finds out. Was that really necessary? Didn't he tell her there was a nursery nearby, a super cheap one? He could have given her a bunch of cuttings himself, whole plants even. In fact, he gives her a hardy cactus already budding with fuchsia flowers. Nat reluctantly places it by the door. It's a marvellous specimen and its mere presence soaks up all the attention.

The change to the yard is undeniable. The sprouts take root and grow by the day. Roberta, the old woman in the small yellow cottage, comes over and offers her enthusiastic congratulations. Right away, Nat feels drawn to her. She must have been quite beautiful when young. Something of that beauty can be appreciated in the slender lines of her nose and mouth. Her eyes, though, are the most striking: dark, penetrating, warm. Her hair, fine and very white, spreads over her head like a light mist. The woman heaps praise on Nat's work. She tells her that since she arrived, it's all very different, and change – all change – is always good.

'Bad thing, stagnant water,' she winks.

Nat realises the woman thinks she's bought the house. No one in their right mind would go to all this trouble for a rented hovel.

Even a crazy old lady can see that.

The words another person wrote before her, words chosen with care, words selected from all the myriad possibilities and arranged in a singular fashion among the infinity of discarded combinations, these words impose themselves on her. If she wants to do her job well – and she does – she must take every one of those choices into account. But that line of thinking leads to exhaustion and paralysis. By dissecting the language so conscientiously, she strips it of meaning. Each word becomes an enemy and translation the closest thing to duelling with a version of her text that both predates hers, and is better. She's exasperated by her slow progress. Is it the heat, the solitude, the lack of confidence, the fear? Or is it simply – and maybe she should just admit it – her ineptitude, her clumsiness?

She puts the dog bowl in the kitchen so Sieso gets used to coming inside. Sometimes she manages to get him to stay a little longer, lying down beside her. It's never for long, he never seems entirely relaxed, but for Nat it's an accomplishment: having him there, close enough to touch. When she runs her palm over his back, she senses, under the fur, the agitation that dominates him still, a continuous pulsing flow. He jumps at the slightest noise or movement she makes and is off like a shot. Then she has to earn his trust all over again.

That's exactly what happens one morning, when she sees him tense, jump up, whine softly, and go outside. A few seconds go by before Nat hears the Jeep come to a stop and footsteps on the gravel. It's the landlord, here to collect the rent. In cash, like they agreed. Like they agreed? Actually, she thinks angrily, she never agreed to anything. According to him, that's how they had to do it, if she wanted him to give her a deal, that is. No bank transfers or deposits, he decreed. She didn't care either way, right? So now, because she'd tried to avoid an argument, she has him here inside the house, having rapped on the door, entering before Nat even has a chance to answer. Before she can even stand to greet him, he's looking around, evaluating the changes she's made, a half-smile playing on his lips. Such a skinny man, Nat thinks, so insignificant, yet he has the power to contaminate the house in just a few seconds. She takes out the rent money, hands it over to him in an envelope.

'You should let me know next time,' she says. 'I might not

have been here.' 'Bah, don't worry about that. If you're not here one day, I'll come the next.'

He's also brought her the bills. Electricity and gas, which are monthly, and the water, to be paid every three months. The fact that she's only been there a month is irrelevant. The house was unoccupied before her, he says, so that bill, the water bill, is also her sole responsibility. The amount is outrageous. Just holding it, Nat's hand shakes.

'I told you already that the tub faucet leaks. There's no way I've used this much.' 'What are you implying, that I should pay it?'

'I'm just saying that it wasn't me. It's the faucet.'

'Not the faucet's fault, girl. You're the one living here, aren't you? Well, you should have fixed it.'

She should have. Nat knows he is partly right, but she told him about it the first day and he did nothing, or rather, the solution he gave – fixing it himself – hadn't convinced her. She could have asked someone else for help. Píter, for instance, though he would have criticised her acquiescence. Or she could have simply called a plumber, like everyone else does. In any case, she'd been avoiding it. In the end, she got used to the sound of constant dripping. She turned her attention to other things. And now here she is, literally left holding the problem.

Fine, she says. She'll pay the bill with next month's rent, if that's okay with him. The landlord grunts in the affirmative, not the least grateful for her concession. Without another word, he leaves in a huff.

Nat remembers only later that she never asked him about Sieso's shots, or the bed she wants him to take away. Doesn't matter, she tells herself quickly, it's not that important. The mere risk of prolonging their encounters is so upsetting that she prefers not to bring it up. She'll deal with it herself.

A plumber in Petacas agrees to come out to La Escapa the next day. That same morning, while still stretching in bed, Nat hears a noise in the bathroom. At first, she thinks Sieso has gotten loose and come in to look for her, but she dresses quickly, heart pounding, because those are human sounds, not animal: footsteps, a bag dropping, a weak clearing of the throat, more footsteps on the tile. Nat shouts *who's there*, she looks, terrified, into the bathroom. When she sees the landlord, she cries out again. It's fear at first, then indignation, and quickly, fear again. *What are you doing here*, she shouts over and over, on the edge of hysteria.

The landlord laughs, tells her to calm down. 'Easy, girl, it's me, it's fine.'

He says he's come to fix the faucet. Needed fixing, didn't it? Hadn't she said so? He thought she wasn't home, or that she was asleep, because he didn't hear anything when he pulled up.

'But you can't come in without warning me first! You shouldn't even have a key! Who told you that you can open the door whenever you want?'

He laughs again.

'Don't get lawyerly with me, girl. I already said I thought you weren't home.'

He explains that the house was on his way, so he decided to come by early, later he has some other errands in La Escapa, and this way he doesn't waste the morning. He tells her he'll be done in a few minutes anyway, it's a simple repair, anyone could have fixed that faucet. Any man, he specifies, because she obviously wasn't capable of it. Nat can't stop shouting. She insists, her voice warped by nerves, that he doesn't have permission to come inside like this, that he must never do it again. The landlord purses his lips, hardens his eyes.

'What, you think I'm going to rape you or something?'

He looks her up and down with scorn. Then he turns back to the tub, bends down, muttering, fiddling with his tools. He says – under his breath, although Nat hears him perfectly clear – that he's sick of women. The more you give them, he says, the worse they think it is. They're all crazy, they're neurotic. He continues working and complaining. Nat remains frozen in the doorway. Then she goes out onto the porch and waits there for him to finish, still shaking.

'Done,' he says a little while later. 'See? Wasn't a big deal.' He leaves without saying goodbye.

Still seated on the porch floor, Nat tries to suppress her anxiety, restrain herself from calling the police, or Píter, or whomever, hugging her knees until the upheaval slowly gives way to a kind of calm. Even so, she forgets to notify the plumber, who turns up a few hours later and, despite not having anything to fix, charges her for the trip nevertheless.

'I put off another client to come out here. This place is a pain to get to,' he apologises. Nat doesn't argue. It's true. This place is decidedly a pain.

Píter has brought over some vegetables he bought from the German. It's too much for just him, he explains, but the German, very astute, always sells them like this, in big batches, so they don't rot. There are radishes, zucchini, cucumbers, tomatoes, and some bulbs Nat can't identify. The German? she asks, still wounded by Píter's comments. She seems to recall a guy, not that tall, with a mustache and glasses, awkward, dark and shy, a guy she's passed a few times, someone who's barely mumbled hello, never meeting her eye.

'Oh, thanks,' she says flatly. 'But I don't know what I'll do with all of it.'

Ratatouille? Chilled soup? Vegetable lasagne? There are a million recipes, Píter replies. Why doesn't she stop wasting her time with the dog and make something for the two of them? He can contribute as well, a main course. They could have dinner at his place and he could show her his studio. Tomorrow. How's that sound?

Nat accepts. He's invited her by too many times for her to keep putting it off. This time, though, it's different. This time, it's a proper invitation: dinner, drinks, chat, all that implies. Nat isn't naïve, she knows the possible implications of Píter's invitation and although something inside of her still resists – a subtle but persistent aversion – she needs to surrender. Ever since the landlord invaded her house, her sleep has been restless; she thinks she hears the key turning in the lock, the door opening, footsteps approaching. She hasn't wanted to say anything to Píter because she knows what he'll say: she should report him to the police right away. He'll be unyielding and will condemn her passivity and indolence. She would rather say nothing, keep it all to herself. And yet, being so isolated isn't easy, it's good to have a friend, otherwise she'll go crazy. She wonders if all she wants is friendship, or protection, too, and if she would feel the same relief – or the same unease – if the invitation came from a woman. A female friend would fit the bill, surely, but wouldn't do much to alleviate her sense of defencelessness. Anyway, she tells herself, Píter is the one expressing his desire to protect her. She just has to let him do it. She isn't asking anything for anything he isn't already willing to give her.

Píter's house is on the west side of La Escapa, some ten minutes from Nat's. It's a pretty wooden building with a pitched roof, wide windows, and garden beds. The inside is cool and pleasant, and although the space is cluttered with objects, they all appear to occupy a particular place and have a precise function and purpose. When Nat enters the foyer, Píter's dog comes over to sniff at the pan in her hands.

'Stuffed zucchini,' she announces.

Píter laughs loudly, taking her arm and leading her to the kitchen. A similar pan sits on the counter, the same dish. They laugh, the dog wags her tail and squeezes between them, looking for a pat. 'My Funny Valentine' is playing, maybe the Chet Baker version, but Nat doesn't ask – she never asks those sorts of questions. Píter pours her a glass of wine and brings her down to the basement to show off his workshop. There, too, everything is carefully organised; ready, even, for an exhibit: plans and sketches, glass fragments in baskets and boxes – classified by colour – tools hung on the wall, a broad table with a half-finished windowpane and soldering irons suspended from the ceiling. Nat would prefer to poke around on her own, but she listens politely to Píter's explanations as he details, step by step, the stained-glass fabrication process. A simple stained-glass window, he says, improves any house, no matter how humble. Of course, if they commission him for something more formal, or even institutional, he doesn't say no, but he prefers to work on a small scale, for regular people. Nat moves in to examine the windowpane on the table. Lambs and doves dance around a leafy tree. The multiple shades of green used for the leaves creates an impression of disorder, or imbalance. Nat isn't sure she likes it. Viewed up close, the composition strikes her as conventional and rather unrefined.

'I was inspired by Chagall for this series. By the windows he made for the University of Hadassah, in Jerusalem. You know them, I suppose, very famous...'

Nat doesn't have the faintest idea, but she nods anyway. She turns toward the wall, where other windows in the series lean, finished and ready to be installed. They're for a library, Peter explains, that's why he's put verses on them: by Pablo Neruda, Mario Benedetti, and Wisława Szymborska. Nat reads them slowly before asking:

'And you can make a living with these?'

She immediately regrets the words. It's the kind of loaded question she hates to be asked. But Píter doesn't seem to be bothered; quite the opposite, in fact. He answers gladly, with pride.

'Of course.'

He spends very little on materials, he says. He uses mostly recycled glass. He actually finds the most valuable pieces in the trash. He is committed to austerity as a way of life. His mottos: throw nothing away; reuse everything you can; respect the Earth; minimal consumption, maximum depth.

'I have the feeling we're rather alike in that respect,' he says, while inside Nat, a swift twinge of concern alights.

During dinner, her suspicions abate. Maybe it's the wine, but it's also Píter's affability; he proves to be warm and even witty, making her laugh like she hasn't laughed in a long time.

Nevertheless, she watches him from the corner of her eye as they clear the table and he opens another bottle of wine, finding that there's something about him she just doesn't like, something that makes her hang back. It's not his physical appearance. In fact, his body is solid and attractive. His brawn is undoubtedly erotic. And he undoubtedly goes out of his way to please: he's charming, a good neighbour, knows about books, music, and movies, everything one supposes is interesting in certain circles – her circle. So? Nat wonders why he lives alone, why he hasn't mentioned a woman yet, dismisses the possibility that he might be gay. Then she takes the glass he offers her and smiles. She forces herself to brush away her prejudices.

They go out into the yard to look at the stars. The night is clear and the Milky Way looms in the darkness, pure and immense. The tips of the blades of grass gleam, bathed in the nocturnal light, swaying, rocked by the wind. The dog sits off to the side, drooling, beautiful and majestic despite her age. They three observe the sky in silence. So pretty, Nat murmurs as, perplexingly, she simultaneously thinks: my period. When the moment comes, she can tell him she has her period.

He turns toward her, scrutinises her with a different sort of smile. 'Can I ask you something?'

'Of course.'

'Why did you come to La Escapa?'

Nat stutters. Hadn't she already answered that? Why does everyone assume she has a hidden motive? She doesn't reply, but finishes her the last of her wine. Píter apologises. He doesn't mean to be nosy, he says. She doesn't have to tell him anything if she doesn't want to, but, if she does want to talk, he'd be delighted to hear her story.

'I left my job,' she says at last. 'I couldn't take any more.' 'What did you do?'

Nat pulls back. She doesn't want to go into detail. It was an office job, she says. Commercial translations, correspondence with foreign clients, stuff like that. Not badly paid work, but definitely a far cry from her interests. Píter lights a cigarette, squints with the first drag.

'Well, you're brave.' 'Why?'

'Because no one quits their job these days.'

Nat is irritated by the praise. She might have accepted it, under other circumstances, but now she's flooded with the desire to resist. Coming from Píter, the compliment sounds poisonous. Or maybe, she thinks, it's her perception, blurred by the alcohol, that makes her take it that way, twisted.

No, she isn't brave, she retorts. She didn't go voluntarily. Not entirely. Does he want to know the real story? Píter leans in. Of course.

She stole something. She'd stolen, not out of necessity, but impulse. She never did comprehend why she did it. It wasn't a for the thrill of the challenge, definitely not for greed. The object was just there and she simply took it. It belonged to one of the company's partners. To one of the partner's wives, to be precise, something valuable she left behind on a visit. Later, returning it got complicated. Even if she'd wanted to – and of course she had – it became impossible to restore order. She could return the stolen object, but not without consequences. She chose to keep quiet. They caught her in the end. They called her aside, they behaved with discretion. She had always been a good employee, qualified and responsible. They only asked why she had done it, and she couldn't answer. Well, they said, sometimes we don't know why we do what we do, right? Such benevolence made her suspicious. She couldn't believe that a simple warning was all she was going to get. Maybe someone had interceded on her behalf. Someone who, later, would make clear exactly what she owed them. Her absolution now had a price, and she wasn't sure she wanted to pay it. She didn't want to stay where, from then on, they would be looking over her shoulder, knowing she had something to hide. Where, if she kept working, it was thanks to her superiors' compassion and generosity, and under new terms of an unwritten contract.

Píter listens and nods, deeply concentrated on her story, but when Nat is finished, he simply repeats his initial compliment: she's brave, whatever she might say. She's been brave enough to break with everything. Someone else in her position would have kept her head down, he's sure of that. She shouldn't feel guilty. Sometimes, certain mistakes lead us to the right thing, a change of course or even a revelation. Isn't it a good thing that she's here now, starting a new life?

They toast and drink, but a shadow has fallen over them, polluting the air. A new life, Nat thinks, and immediately feels ashamed. Everything she has said is true; and yet, because of the way she told it – her choice of words, cadence, pauses, and circumventions – it's topped with a halo of falseness that she finds repellent. Her need to justify herself, she thinks, is pathetic.

Seeing her wilt, Píter kindly changes the subject, asks her about her current work, about the translation. It's her first assignment, she explains. Her first literary translation, she clarifies. She's never done anything like it before. In fact, you might say she's being put to the test. The publishing house that offered her the job has faith in her abilities, but it represents

71

a qualitative leap, that's for sure. Commercial translation is straightforward and this...well, what she's aiming for is the essence, the very heart of language.

Píter is interested in the book itself, less so in theoretical digressions. What's it about, he asks. Is it a novel? Essay? What? It's impossible to explain, Nat says. There's no unfolding plot that can be summed up in a one or two sentences. They're theatrical pieces, very short, almost schematic, philosophical in tone. The author didn't write them in her mother tongue, but in the language of the country where she lived in exile, so the language is very rudimentary, even flat. At first Nat thought this would be advantageous, but it's revealing itself to be a challenge. Now she finds herself obliged to decipher whether each unexpected or ambiguous word is an error based on a lack of knowledge of the language, or if it's an intended effect resulting from intense consideration. There's no way to know.

'And you can't ask the author?'

Nat shakes her head, irked. The woman died, which, maybe is for the best. This way, she's spared the disappointment of witnessing the mess Nat is making of her book.

Píter smiles, looks back up at the sky. Nice profession, he says. Translation. Interesting and useful, he adds. Necessary. He sets aside his glass and, with a napkin, wipes his dog's mouth. The docile animal lets him do it, and in that placidity – and in Píter's manner – Nat sees great gentleness, but a kind of gentleness that is artificial, calculated. Sieso would never let anyone clean him like that. Maybe that's why Píter does it, to highlight the difference between the animals. When he's done, he fills Nat's glass again. Fuzzily, Nat thinks: he's getting me drunk. In the distance, a word takes shape – *this* – and then a complete sentence: *this is how the charades begin.*

Why doesn't Píter tell her anything about himself? Why does he just poke around, attempting to draw her out. Where does he get the authority to give her advice? Time for me to go, she announces, then realises, upon standing, just how dizzy she is. She tries to dissimulate her wobbling as Píter takes her to the bathroom, where she stays a long time, until the alcohol's effects have somewhat dissipated.

It's very late when he offers to take her back to her house. He drops her off at her front door and asks her if she'll be all right. Nat nods and thanks him. Píter brushes her cheek softly, bids her goodnight – get some rest, he says – and that's it. Nat is surprised, disappointed even. Wasn't he going to kiss her, or at least try? He wasn't going to try to take her to bed? Isn't that the predictable thing, what's expected from a man? Why the Sam Cooke and the Miles Davis and so much wine, why the Milky Way? She had her excuse all ready for nothing. But then, would she have wanted anything different? No, definitely not, but she doesn't want this either, not the stumbling around in the entryway, the clumsy steps, the vertigo, and the total solitude of the shut-up house. Nat lurches toward bed and then hears something, a sound approaching from the shadows. She feels her heart dropping to the floor, until she realises that Sieso is licking her trembling hand. It is the first time the dog has shown her any sign of affection, a greeting. Excited, she crouches, cries, talks to him.

'You scared me!'

She hugs him. His coarse fur gets in her nose and eyes, but still she hugs him, so tight that eventually Sieso wriggles away with a growl.

73

Her relationship with Píter becomes closer after that night. Having revealed certain things to him, Nat is at a disadvantage, but this asymmetry doesn't worry her: she hasn't told him everything – not even close. His attitude hasn't changed following her confidences. If anything, he is even more affable, more affectionate. They text each other throughout the day and Nat often visits him at home; she no longer needs an invitation, going over when she feels like it or is bored. Following her intuition, she steers clear of information she believes inconvenient to share. She doesn't tell him, for instance, about Sieso's gradual progress or her fear of the landlord. What for? Píter's tendency to get insert himself into everything, his patronising tone – the supposed voice of experience – because he's a man, because he's older, because he's been in La Escapa longer, because he's friends with all the people whose names Nat barely knows – doesn't seem serious enough to impede their friendship.

What became obvious during the dinner – that there is no sexual attraction between them – contributes, paradoxically, to their closeness. And yet, Píter's disinterest sets off alarm bells for Nat: a sign that she is starting to lose a power that, until now, she had unconsciously possessed. Like money, she says to herself, erotic capital also imperceptibly erodes over time, we only become aware of it when it's gone, and she scrutinises herself in the mirror with merciless eyes, evaluating the parts of her body or face where the flaw might reside. True, she has let herself go since she arrived in La Escapa. Her hair is messy and coarse, the work clothes do nothing for her, and the hours spent in the sun, instead of bronzing her skin, have left it red and parched. But there must be something else. Something to do with age, or the pressing weight of time, not its passing.

She'd rather not think about it. As with so many other things, she sets the idea aside, quarantined.

Sometimes she has the sense that the landlord has used his key again, to enter the house in her absence. There is no demonstrable proof, nothing out of place, no evidence of his presence, but the mere possibility – a real possibility, as she has seen – is weighty enough to distress her. She forces herself to be rational. She must dispel her suspicions and not obsess. Yet all it takes is closing her eyes and relaxing her consciousness for the landlord's spectre to waltz in, in the shape of a nightmare.

In a recurring dream, she discovers a window beside her bed, a new window that appears overnight. The exterior blinds are half closed and a pair of white curtains partially obscure the view outside. Through the window, or what little can be seen through it, she perceives an unfamiliar but perfectly realistic landscape. The scene is not always the same: sometimes there are snow-capped mountains under a sooty sky, or a rough sea, or blocks of very tall buildings on the outskirts of a city, all their lights on. When, fascinated, she tries to sit up to get a better look, she realises she is tied to the headboard – or the box frame or legs – with ribbons knotted at her wrists. They don't seem like much, the ribbons, but she is completely immobilised by them. Nat doesn't know who has tied her up, nor when. She observes the knots pressing on her veins, the chafing on her skin, her fingers that tingle with the lack of circulation. Fear takes hold. At that moment, she hears the front door opening and a man coming inside with slow, scuffling footsteps he makes no effort to conceal. Nat wonders where Sieso could be, why he hasn't barked to warn her. Never leaving the bed, she can somehow see the man making his way through every room in the house – a much bigger house than she'd thought, with a multitude of rooms she didn't know were there: storage closets, attics, small rooms inside other rooms. She sees the man, the man's back, his bare, staunch neck, watches as it enters every space, contaminating it with his very presence. But she cannot see his face. The man comes to the side of her bed. Something in her throat goes spongy, muffling her scream. Nat is suffocating.

She wakes up sweaty, limbs heavy and gums parched. The night sounds mix with her still-confused senses: a horse's nervous whinny, the hoot of a brown owl, dense cricket song, and the dogs, always the dogs, their overlapping barks.

But worse are the noises she discovers, even seeks, inside the house. Every day, every night, dreaming or not. Creaks and squeals, air whistling through the shutters, the fan's hum, Sieso's toenails click-clacking on the old wooden porch, pacing around the stake. None of the noises are associated with the landlord, but her guard is up. When he comes with the second month's bills, he knocks on the front door. Nat's relief is so great that she pays without complaint. This is better, she tells herself. Don't ask for anything, finish up quickly, then be free of his face until the following month.

She can spend entire days roaming and, except for work crews, meet almost no one: just the gypsy collecting scrap metal or running errands, or Joaquín – Roberta's husband – or the German, driving his van back and forth to Petacas, presumably to sell vegetables from his garden. If it weren't for Píter, she might not speak to anyone for days. Now that she's not a novelty, not even the shopgirl takes an interest in her. She simply rings up Nat's shopping, her eyes glued to the TV mounted in the corner. Her boredom gives off a whiff of despair. Nat watches her crack her knuckles, lost in thought, humming under her breath. Her still-adolescent face contains the template for how she will be when she's fifty or sixty, when she's plagued by the same migraines as her mother. Nat would like to be kind to her, but can't think of anything to say.

Sometimes she goes with Píter to Gordo's bar, a warehouse with an asbestos ceiling lit by a single bulb emanating blue-tinged light. They drink bottles of beer with the men who stop in – farmers and bricklayers, mostly – people who discuss matters about which Nat has nothing to add. Píter chats with them easily, though she has the impression that he's acting, getting down on their level. Sometimes Gordo charges extra, sometimes he doesn't charge at all, and no one's allowed to argue.

There's always a hint of aggression, of provocation, in the way he jokes with his customers but they all laugh it off. Nat does, too. She would never go to that place alone, but with Píter it's different.

One night, the wind changes direction and the temperature drops. Nat is reading on the porch; at first she gets a cardigan, then goes inside, still too chilly. Hot, fat raindrops promptly begin to fall and within a couple of minutes the downpour begins, raising a new, encouraging scent from the wet earth. Nat is as happy as a child. She feels like she has made it to the end of a phase, the first and most challenging, and that the rain marks the start of a new – and more promising – stage. But her joy is short-lived: just as long as it takes for the leaks and a swiftly widening puddle to appear. Nat runs for some buckets; when she returns, hair and clothes soaked through, mud has already started to form inside the house. Incredible, she thinks. What does one do in these situations? And how hadn't she noticed before? Hadn't she seen the yellow stains on the ceiling a thousand times? What did she think they were? She spends half the night emptying buckets and putting them back, until the storm wanes and she can lie down to rest. She sleeps for intervals, afraid the rain will start up again, knowing that, this time, she'll have no choice but to call the landlord. But the sky is radiant in the morning, not a trace of clouds. Can she put the call off? At least until the next time he comes with the bills? With any luck, it won't rain again before then; better to wait, not wake the dragon too soon. She knows she's making excuses to avoid the problem, but, she tells herself, they aren't really excuses, they're actual facts: the sky doesn't threaten more rain, it was just a passing August rainstorm, nothing to worry about for now.

Her forecast is correct: no drops fall over the coming days. She can almost manage to forget the issue, but not quite. Whenever she looks up, she is confronted by the stains, which look like limescale or urine and gross her out. When the month ends and the landlord shows up in his grubby overalls, Nat shows him the stains. He squints to inspect them. She tells him what happened the night of the downpour, about the puddles and buckets. She explains that this is why the wood floor is rotting. This is irrefutable proof, she thinks. He cannot deny the evidence.

'Well, girl, it doesn't rain like that every day.'

'Not every day, no. But it could happen again. I mean, it'll definitely rain this autumn, right? Maybe not as hard, but the leaks are there and...' She falters. 'The floor is getting ruined...'

The landlord looks at her breasts as she speaks. He's doing it on purpose, Nat thinks. To destabilise her, she thinks. Humiliate her. Lip curling, he says the rotting floor isn't her problem. Not her house, is it? She's just a renter, he repeats, a renter who has done nothing but complain ever since she arrived.

'What do you want me to do? You think the shitty rent you pay is enough for me get bogged down in a bunch of home improvements?'

Nat, furious, is incapable of expressing her anger. She wants to be forceful. Instead, she just sounds hesitant and scared.

'So the next time it pours, I'm just supposed to put out buckets?' 'Exactly!'

He points a finger at her and she weakens. Her throat burns, a scorching sensation that reaches her eyeballs. Is she going to cry? She cannot let that happen. She must contain the urge, no matter what.

'I think...all of this just isn't... I don't think this is normal.'

'No? Don't think it's normal, do you? And just what do you think is normal, girl? To come out to the middle of the country and expect a cushy city life?'

He begins to speak in plural then, throwing his arms about, pacing in circles.

'You women are all the same. You think this is all starry skies at night and little lambs baaing in the morning. Then you're on about the mosquitos, the rain, the weeds. Look, I already brought the price way down. Did I bring it down or not? Or don't you remember now? When you've had a problem, haven't I fixed it? Didn't I fix the faucet? Oh, you thought that was horrible, too. Can't understand you women. Look, I got a lot more important things to do. Give me my money and get off my back.'

Nat pays him and he leaves, slamming the door behind him. She cries then, full of rage because she cannot understand what it is about the landlord that so terrifies her. A rude, small-minded man with no actual power over her. Is he not clearly inferior? Uneducated, dirty, and poor, what damage can he do? Why does he have such an effect on her? She cries and, at the same time, tries to convince herself that maybe there won't be more leaks, maybe putting out a few buckets when it rains is fine, maybe that was an unusual storm, maybe it's not really that big of a deal, maybe she can hold out for a few months. It isn't her house, after all, she'll end up moving out sooner or later. In the meantime, it's better to be chill, not stress, not let herself get upset. This is how she will defeat him, how she will stay on top.

But the stains continue to speak for themselves. This time, it's the German who sees them when he comes around, offering her a crate of vegetables. He sets the box down in the entryway and he stops at the ruined floorboards. He looks up and examines the ceiling.

'You've got leaks.'

He has an odd way of speaking, knocking his syllables together, like he's in a rush or being abrupt. Without meeting her eye, he asks for a chair and climbs up for a closer look. Nat notices his boots – sturdy and worn, the same pair he had on at the meeting – as he explains the cause of the problem.

'Looks like it's been like this a long time. There are probably a decent number of broken tiles up there. You'd need to check and see if they can be fixed, but I doubt it. When the leaks are superficial, you can just cover the tiles with bitumen or lime, but I'm afraid this is more complicated. What'd your landlord say?'

'That it only leaks when there's heavy rain. That it's not his problem. And that he's not going to do anything.'

The German gets down from the chair, shakes his head.

'As soon as it rains again, even just a sprinkle, this will all flood again. I could fix it for you.'

Nat appreciates that he doesn't comment on the landlord's stance. She likes that he doesn't judge her, that he doesn't deem the situation as fair or unfair, doesn't urge her to argue or defend her position. The German sticks to the facts, sees the situation head-on, without his own interpretation. This attitude is precisely what gives her license to vent and complain.

'It's ridiculous that I have to fix it. He should do it, right? It's his house.'

'Yeah. His house, but your problem. I can help you, seriously. I know how to fix it.'

To prove this, he describes the process in detail: first, they need to evaluate how far the breakage goes; then, look for similar tiles and retile the affected area. Finally, channel the runoff with either grating or gutters so it doesn't happen again, they'd see about that later. But they're not friends, Nat thinks. She'll have to pay him. And how much could something like that cost? She doesn't have much money, but also won't accept any favours. She doesn't distrust him, but she doesn't want to owe him anything.

'I don't know if I can afford it,' she says.

The German is silent. She suspects he is about to offer to do it for free. But after a few seconds, he says he understands. He can't estimate how much it will cost before getting started. He doesn't want to fix one problem and cause another. He shrugs and, for the first time, looks at her. There's no disappointment in his eyes. Or resignation. Just a trace of timidity and kindness, maybe a bit of embarrassment. It could be that he's short on cash as well, and saw a chance to earn a little extra income. He seems honest to Nat, but uncouth. All she can do is cross her fingers in hopes that it doesn't rain and buy bigger buckets just in case. She pays for the vegetables, says thanks, and walks him outside.

What happens just two hours later will be meticulously remembered by Nat afterwards, with a need to secure the details in place so as not to forget any of it, to prevent memory from perverting, adulterating, or disguising it.

In her recollection, a word – *droit* – will ring, and a phrase – *le droit de sauver* – from a dialogue she was translating when it happened. *You do not have the right to save whomever you want*, one of the characters protests, and the other replies: *It is not a right, it is a duty!*

Nat is writing those very words when she hears someone call her name. She stands and goes outside and it's him, the German, waiting outside the gate, even though it has stood open since he left. She notices that he's changed his clothes: the faded grey pants for a different pair, clean and blue, the black T-shirt advertising a mechanic's shop for a beige shirt so threadbare it's almost see-through. He doesn't smile, but he isn't serious either. Rather, he gives off the impression that he's focused on something, something he's about to do or say and which doesn't seem directly related to Nat. It occurs to her that he might have forgotten something, or maybe she paid him the wrong amount for the vegetables, or maybe he's going to offer to fix the leaks for free after all, like she'd suspected. His glance at the roof tiles confirms that it's the third option. Predictable, she thinks, although she could have never foreseen what came next.

'I don't want you to get mad,' he says.

He stops at that, studying the roof, squinting in the sunlight. Sieso approaches him slowly, sniffs his pant legs.

'Mad? Why would I get mad?'

It takes him a while to find the words, but this delay doesn't seem to suggest any discomfort with the message, but rather an uncertainty about the use of language itself. Waiting for him to speak, Nat is intrigued, albeit slightly indifferent, as if what he was about to say – or propose, since it's obviously a proposal – didn't concern her.

'I guess you have the right to get mad. It's a risk I'll take.'

It's not a right, it's a duty! Nat thinks, but she smiles, encouraging him to speak. 'Come on, just say it, it's fine.'

He says it. He says he's been alone for a long time. A long time without a woman, he specifies. Living in La Escapa doesn't help. Neither does having a personality like his, cut off and reserved – although he doesn't use those adjectives: he says, simply, *a personality like mine*. It's not like he's unhappy. He's not sad or depressed, that isn't it. But the fact is, men have certain needs. At this his voice cracks a bit, though he steadies it right away. He's not that young anymore, he continues. Some ten or twelve years older than she is – he looks her over, evaluating her. He doesn't feel old, but neither does he have the energy to pick women up. He smiles, embarrassed, and Nat senses that it isn't because of what he means, but the expression *pick up* – so euphemistic and antiquated, out of place. To meet women, he corrects himself. His smile fades. He doesn't want to resort to prostitutes; the ones in Petacas are awful, he says, all of that completely turns him off. She nods mechanically.

It's very simple, really, the German continues. Or it should be. Even though men and women rarely think about it that way. No one dares to speak openly. What's normal – or common – is to have ulterior motives. He thinks that maybe with her, he can cut right to the chase. It's just an intuition he has, maybe she'll misinterpret him and get offended, or she could interpret him correctly and still be offended. He doesn't know her well enough to anticipate how she will react; the only way to know is to just throw it out there. He waits a few seconds, searches her face.

'I can fix your roof in exchange for letting me enter you a little while.'

Later, Nat will repeat these words to herself, over and over, until she is afraid that she's made them up. He doesn't say *in exchange for sleeping with you*. He certainly doesn't use any other expression, more or less offensive, with a similar meaning. He says could she *let him enter*. Not just *enter her* but that she *let him enter*. A strange way to put it, and not the result of a deficient command of the language – he's not German, after all! Let him enter, she repeats to herself. A little while, he said. *A little while.* Nat blinks. She needs to hear more, or perhaps hear it more times in order to understand it. But his attitude – the loose arms, legs apart, the humble, evasive eyes – seems to indicate that he has finished speaking and is now, quite simply, awaiting a response.

'And how would that be, exactly?'

The German looks at her for a moment and tries to smile, but the expression is closer to a wince. Of relief? Of satisfaction, because she isn't angry? Nat wouldn't possibly know how interpret it. Just once, he specifies. A little while, he repeats. The minimum, he says next.

'I won't pester you. I don't want to be a bother. You're not a prostitute, I don't want you to think that I take you for one. It's just – ' He hesitates. 'I'd like to enter you a little while. Simple as that. You lie down and I'll be done fast. That's it. I haven't been with a woman in a long time. My body needs it. I thought I could ask you.'

Later on, Nat will remember these words, too. The coolness of his statements, so short and direct. His concision. He could have said what people usually say in those situations. He could have said, for example, that he liked Nat, that he was attracted to her, that he was risking such a request because he could hardly resist her pull. But those last words – *I thought I could ask you* – mean nothing. He isn't asking Nat because he likes her, but because he thought he could ask her. So, who can he not ask? Who doesn't he ask because – he believes – he cannot?

Subtle but instinctive, Nat allows herself to operate from irritation, as well as impatience. The reaction lasts only an instant, but it is decisive in her refusal, which springs curt and direct from her mouth, catching her almost by surprise.

'Thanks, but no.'

Okay, he says, and calmly makes to leave. He doesn't press, but he doesn't apologise, either.

Nat says goodbye as though, in effect, nothing strange had occurred.

But back at her desk, she is unable to resume her work. It will be several days before she can.

MONA KAREEM
THREE POEMS

Translated from the Arabic by Sara Elkamel

Mona Kareem is the author of three
poetry collections. Her poetry has
been translated into nine languages,
and has appeared (in English) in
POETRY, *Poetry Northwest*, *Michigan
Quarterly*, *Poetry London* and *Modern
Poetry in Translation*, among others.
She is a recipient of a 2021 literary
grant from the National Endowment
for the Arts. Kareem holds a PhD in
Comparative Literature and works as
an assistant professor of Middle East
Studies at Washington University
St. Louis. Her translations include
Ashraf Fayadh's *Instructions Within*
(nominated for a Best Translated
Book Award), Ra'ad Abdulqadir's
Except for this Unseen Thread and
Octavia Butler's *Kindred*.

Sara Elkamel is a poet, journalist
and translator living between her
hometown, Cairo, and New York City.
She holds an MA in arts journalism
from Columbia University, and
an MFA in poetry from New York
University. Elkamel's debut chapbook
Field of No Justice was published by
the African Poetry Book Fund and
Akashic Books in 2021.

The Word's Window

1

He screams for freedom
while his wife shines the same shoe
he kicks her with daily

2

There is a masked man circling
the garden of my silence

3

On the first page of the book,
the publisher surveils
the rights of our death

4

Between a massacre and its playmate
extinguished souls
languish in the void

5

The beggar of nihilism
and the vagrant of existence

6

Poets drench themselves with lies
when they attempt to flee
out the word's window

7
This is what I imagine:
Treacherous friends
and the telegrams of the dead

8
Another clown
kills himself above our smiles

Relics of the Soul

There is nothing left
to celebrate;
all our memories
have splintered.

That's why we forage
for children's heads
to assemble in vases
instead of heaven's incense.

Over here, we leave
a cloud at our door
to signal our departure
is eternal.

Memory is a tourist
perched on a history book
painting a map
of the cosmos.

In one painting, I imagine a cave
free of poverty's cigarettes
and eyes as wide as pain
fixed on a desert
embracing a river
of children's agony.

A Vase and a Moon

I am a vase. A single song is enough to abolish me, enough
to drown the vase in tears. They're dying, they're dying,
they're killing me; all of them conjure death.

To wipe sweat from your eyes is not an easy task.
Do you know that scene with the boy, bawling his lungs breathless
over the bike they confiscated?

The window is open, and there is no moon. There is no moon
in this country; there's an abundance of buildings, the night
nothing more than a black background.

There is no moon.
There is a portrait of you; larger than any moon.

Night falls as the entire world crams itself between you and me...
There is no time to fly; the sun will butcher my wings of wax.

Acknowledgements

We respectfully acknowledge the Gadigal, Burramattagal and Cammeraygal peoples, the traditional owners of the lands where Giramondo's offices are located. We extend our respects to their ancestors and to all First Nations peoples and Elders.

HEAT Series 3 Number 11 has been prepared in collaboration with Ligare Book Printers and Candida Stationery; we thank them for their support.

The Giramondo Publishing Company is grateful for the support of Western Sydney University in the implementation of its book publishing program.

This project has been assisted by the Australian Government through Creative Australia, its principal arts investment and advisory body.

This project is supported by the Copyright Agency's Cultural Fund.

HEAT Series 3
Editor Alexandra Christie
Designer Jenny Grigg
Typesetter Andrew Davies
Copyeditor Aleesha Paz
Marketing Manager Kate Prendergast
Publishers Ivor Indyk and Evelyn Juers
Associate Publisher Nick Tapper

Editorial Advisory Board
Chris Andrews, Mieke Chew, J.M. Coetzee, Lucy Dougan, Lisa Gorton,
Bella Li, Tamara Sampey-Jawad, Suneeta Peres da Costa, Alexis Wright
and Ashleigh Young.

Contact
For editorial enquiries, please email
heat.editor@giramondopublishing.com.
Follow us on Instagram @HEAT.lit and
Twitter @HEAT_journal.

Accessibility
We understand that some formats will not be accessible to all readers.
If you are a reader with specific access requirements, please contact
orders@giramondopublishing.com.

For more information, visit giramondopublishing.com/heat.

Published October 2023
from the Writing and Society Research Centre
at Western Sydney University
by the Giramondo Publishing Company
Locked Bag 1797
Penrith NSW 2751 Australia
www.giramondopublishing.com

This collection © Giramondo Publishing 2023
Typeset in Tiempos and Founders Grotesk Condensed
designed by Kris Sowersby at Klim Type Foundry

Printed and bound by Ligare Book Printers
Distributed in Australia by NewSouth Books

A catalogue record for this book is available from
the National Library of Australia.

HEAT Series 3 Number 11
ISBN: 978-1-922725-10-3
ISSN: 1326-1460